11783434

Roman Satirists in Seventeenth-Century England

Roman Satirists

in Seventeenth-Century England

William Kupersmith

University of Nebraska Press

Lincoln and London

Library of Congress Cataloging
in Publication Data

Kupersmith, William, 1941–
Roman satirists in
seventeenth-century England

Bibliography: p.
Includes index.
1. English poetry—Early modern, 1500–1700—History and criticism.   2. Satire, English—History and
criticism.   3. English poetry—Roman influences.   4.
Latin poetry—Translations into English—History and
criticism.   5. Satire, Latin—Translations into English—History and criticism.   6. English poetry—
Translations from Latin—History and criticism.   7.
Satire, English—Translations from Latin—History
and criticism.   8. Literature, Comparative—English
and Latin.   9. Literature, Comparative—Latin and
English.   10. Imitation (in literature)   I. Title.
PR545.S2K86   1986
821'.4'09   85-1103
ISBN 0-8032-2710-8 (alk. paper)

For My Father and Mother

Contents

Preface

My aim in this study is to discuss every published adaptation of classical Roman verse satire to appear in English during the seventeenth century. I began a decade ago on a larger plan. My original object was to investigate the background to Alexander Pope's *Imitations of Horace* and Samuel Johnson's *London* and *The Vanity of Human Wishes,* and to find out how Roman satire was read by Englishmen in the Restoration and early eighteenth century. Translations and adaptations were to provide but part of the evidence; I also studied Latin editions, commentaries, and critical treatises that would have been read by educated English readers. But in the process of writing this book my focus narrowed to concentrate on the methods used by translators into verse. Of course, the story of how Roman satirists fared in England does not end in 1693 with the publication of Dryden's translation of Juvenal. The great age of adaptation and Imitation of classical satire was to be the following century. Besides the famous Imitations by Pope and by Johnson, there were to be more than forty adaptations of the Roman satirists published between 1709 and 1799. But they will have to be the subjects of another study.

My primary audience includes readers interested in the influence of the classics on English literature, in satire (particularly in "formal verse satire," as it is usually called today) as a literary genre, in the history of translation, and in the development of English verse technique, especially of the heroic couplet. But I have also tried to write a book that students, and general readers might find engaging. All Latin quotations are accompanied by an English translation that is as literal as the differences between Latin and English syntax allow. It is only a crib to the Latin, though where a word-for-word translation resulted in idiomatically impossible English I have altered the construction, for example changing passive voices to active or double negatives to positives. Although the translations are my own, I have not scrupled when stuck for the right turn of phrase to borrow from modern translations and commentaries.[1]

Choosing the proper texts to quote in English and to quote and translate from in Latin presented a particularly vexing problem. Most who study the relationship between classical and modern literature are now aware that simply to adopt a current edition and translation of a classical author (most commonly in the English-speaking world from the Loeb Classical Library) is a sure course to disaster, because the reading preferred by a modern editor may not have been in the editions used in earlier centuries.[2] What appears to have been a gross misunderstanding of Latin may be an accurate translation of a variant reading, and what seems an unwarranted addition by the translator may reflect some early commentator's explanation of what the classical author supposedly meant. So here any Latin text quoted should match those used in the seventeenth century. But how do we know which one to choose? Sometimes the translator's introduction tells us; thus we know that Dryden used the Delphin edition of Juvenal (Paris, 1684), and that Sir Robert Stapleton's 1660 version of Juvenal was based on a text published in Paris in 1644. (Neither, by the way, was a very good choice.) At times a translator's text and the readings and glosses of a particular edition coincide so closely that we can be certain it served as the basis for the translation, as in the case of John Biddle's versions of the first and second satires of Juvenal, which agree completely with Thomas Farnaby's school-text. But more frequently we cannot tell exactly which text—or texts, for there may have been more than one, perhaps a variorum edition offering a variety of readings and commentaries—the translator used. It would be an exhausting, pedantic, and ulti-

mately impossible task to make each quoted classical text match
the accidentals of the edition the seventeenth-century translator
really used. I have adopted a compromise. Accidentals of spelling
and punctuation in quotations from the Roman satirists are based
on modern practice, and because most of my audience will not be
professional Latin scholars, for clarity I have preferred editions in
which consonantal *u* is represented by *v*.[3] Whenever a substantive
variant was clearly present in the text a particular seventeenth-
century writer used, I have adopted it in the Latin quotations. For
example, "Codri" appears instead of "Cordi" in Juvenal, *Satires*
1.2, and "Plance" for "Blande" in 8.40. Similarly, at Horace, *Satires*
1.7.126, I give "rabiosi tempora signi" instead of "campum lusum-
que trigonem."

English writers, on the other hand, appear as they do in the
editions cited in the body of the text or in the notes. Where no
modern edition exists, as in the case of Barksted, Holyday, and
Wood, the only recourse was the first edition.[4] But when a critical
modern edition is available it is quoted, and where there is more
than one an old-spelling text has been preferred if possible. When
referring to seventeenth-century writers, I spell their names
according to the form given first in the *Dictionary of National
Biography*. When line numbers appear in the text I use them to
cite English poetry, otherwise I give page or folio. Classical
poetry is cited by the usual verse numbers.

The choice to quote translations of many different passages
from Roman satire was quite deliberate, even though it rendered
comparison between one translator and another more difficult.
Reading translations of the same passage over and over again can
be excruciatingly boring. However well differences in style stand
out, the monotony of content is soporific. So I have tried use a
variety of passages, most of them ones I enjoy (after all, the author
has to stay awake too), but which I thought displayed the particular abilities of the translator I was discussing. Of course such old
favorites as the conclusion of the tenth satire of Juvenal make a
number of appearances.

While writing this book I tried to avoid generalizations and
theoretical statements about what a good translation ought to be.

My reluctance was not due to ignorance of what critics—from Matthew Arnold to D. S. Carne-Ross and George Steiner—have written, but to a desire to find a way of discussing and evaluating seventeenth-century English adaptations that would be empirical. While reading I generally kept an eye out for passages that seemed remarkable or at least representative, then I compared them to the Latin originals, which served in a sense as my control group. After comparing a number of passages I would try to judge how well the English version succeeded both as an original poem and as a reproduction of its Roman model. Three qualities seemed crucial to success or failure.

The decasyllabic couplet was nearly the unanimous choice of seventeenth-century translators and Imitators—perhaps because of their training at school—so a good many of the successful versions were the result of superior technique. But diction and tone were critical, too, and unfortunately the notion that satire was spoken by satyrs or inspired by the "pedestrian muse" led to some slapdash work. Allusions to social life, customs, religion, and morality, as well as to particular people, were a tough challenge for adaptors trying to steer a course between the shoals of obscurity and anachronism.

I am grateful to the staffs of the University of Iowa Library, the Beinecke Rare Book and Manuscript Collection at Yale University, the British Library, and the Bodleian Library, where I did most of the research for this study. Additionally, I want to thank John Riely, Howard D. Weinbrot, and Alvaro Ribeiro for a number of favors. Antonius J. Schulze Walgern was an invaluable research assistant, who saved me from a lot of embarrassing blunders. Two anonymous readers for the University of Nebraska Press pointed out some more errors. Adrienne Mayor's superb editing eliminated a host of repetitions, awkward expressions, digressions, and mistranslations. Of course those that remain are my responsibility. The Graduate College of the University of Iowa provided an Old Gold Summer Fellowship that enabled me to begin this project, and a one-semester Developmental Leave to finish it. Even when there were oceans between us, Katherine V. Frank was a wonderfully appreciative audience for early versions of most of these chapters.

Ben Jonson, Juvenal, and Horace

Sorting the orders of precedence among the fleas and the lice of the kingdom of letters may seem at first glance a waste of time, but very minor writers have their uses, and not only for the literary entomologist. Like social climbers aping their betters, minor poets will die first rather than be seen in anything but the height of literary fashion, which makes them infallible guides to the literary tastes of a period. Anyone trying to pass for a poet will be careful to produce whatever contemporary taste considers the essence of true poetry. In Queen Elizabeth's time it would be sonnet sequences, in the mid-seventeenth century metaphysical odes, in the 1960s and 1970s the neurotic howlings of the "confessional" poets. Great writers, in contrast, have a bad habit of being original and thus interfering with the orderly development of literary history.

Translators are no exception. If one accepts, as everyone in the seventeenth century seems to have done, that the Roman verse satirists are models for poets writing satire in English, then a study of English translations and adaptations should enable us to follow what seventeenth-century English readers thought about Roman satire, and what methods they believed would be most effective in reproducing its effects in English. Second- and third-rate poets often failed to achieve what they set out to do, but what they were trying to do is usually easy to discern—indeed, they leave behind more evidence of their intentions than do accomplished poets who have learned from Horace to conceal their art.

Yet it is auspicious that we can begin our survey with a major author who was both a Horatian and a Juvenalian, Ben Jonson. The influence of the classics on Jonson is an enormous subject; here I shall discuss only passages adapted from the satires of Juvenal and Horace that are long enough to be treated independently.

[I]

Jonson was a devoted reader of Juvenal. He owned a fifteenth-century manuscript of the satires and copies of the Ceruto edition of 1599 and the Lubin edition of 1603, and incorporated many quotations of Juvenal into his plays.[1] His only substantial translation from Juvenal into verse occurs in his tragedy *Sejanus* (1603), where Jonson turned Juvenal's account in the tenth satire of the fall of Sejanus, Tiberius' favorite who became virtual ruler of the Roman Empire, straight into dialogue. The original, in the order Jonson adapted it, reads

> . . . descendunt statuae restemque sequuntur,
> ipsas deinde rotas bigarum inpacta securis
> caedit et inmeritis franguntur crura caballis;
> iam strident ignes, iam follibus atque caminis
> ardet adoratum populo caput et crepat ingens
> Seianus; deinde ex facie toto orbe secunda
> fiunt urceoli pelves sartago matellae. . . .
>   ". . . curramus praecipites et,
> dum iacet in ripa, calcemus Caesaris hostem—
> sed videant servi, ne quis neget et pavidum in ius
> cervice obstrica dominum trahat.". . .
>   . . . gaudent omnes. "quae labra, quis illi
> vultus erat! numquam, si quid mihi credis, amavi
> hunc hominem!" "sed quo cecidit sub crimine? quisnam
> delator? quibus indicibus, quo teste probavit?"
> "nil horum: verbosa et grandis epistula venit
> a Capreis." "bene habet; nil plus interrogo." sed quid
> turba Remi? sequitur fortunam ut semper et odit
> damnatos. idem populus, si Nortia Tusco
> favisset, si oppressa foret secura senectus
> principis, hac ipsa Seianum diceret hora
> Augustum . . .   [58–64, 85–88, 67–77]

[The statues fall and follow the rope, the axe strikes and cuts the wheels from the chariot and the legs of the innocent horses are broken. Now the fires crackle, now the bellows and forges make the head adored by the people blaze and great Sejanus cracks; from whose face—second in the entire world—will come basins, jugs, a frying pan, pisspots. . . . "Let us run quickly and kick the enemy of Caesar as he lies on the riverbank. But let the slaves see us, lest one deny it and drag his terrified master into court with a rope round his neck." . . . All rejoice. "What lips, what a face that man had! I never—if you ever believe anything I say—liked him." "But for what crime did he perish? Who was the accuser and who were the witnesses—by whose testimony was the charge proved?" "By none of these. A long windy letter came from Capri." "That's fine. I'll ask no more." But what of the Roman mob? They follow fortune and hate the condemned. The same people, if Nortia had favored her Tuscan and if the carefree old-age of the ruler had been cut off, today would have hailed Sejanus Emperor.]

In Jonson's tragedy these lines are put into the mouth of Terentius, one of Sejanus' followers, as he reports his leader's fall, telling how the mob, like rowdy supporters at a football match, rush to destroy the relics of their fallen idol:

They fill'd the *capitoll*, and POMPEI's circke:
Where, like so many mastiues, biting stones,
As if his statues now were sensiue growne
Of their wild furie, first, they teare them downe:
Then fastning ropes, drag them along the streets,
Crying in scorne, this, this was that rich head
Was crown'd with gyrlands, and with odours, this
That was in *Rome* so reuerenced! Now
The fornace, and the bellowes shall to worke,
The great SEIANVS crack, and piece, by piece,
Drop i' the founders pit . . .

Lepidus, a senator, interrupts indignantly:

. . . O, popular rage!

And Terentius continues:

The whilst, the *Senate*, at the temple of *Concord*,
Make haste to meet again, and thronging cry,
Let vs condemne him, tread him downe in water,
While he doth lie vpon the banke; away:
Where some, more tardie, cry vnto their bearers,
He will be censur'd ere we come, runne knaues;
And vse that furious diligence, for feare
Their bond-men should informe against their slacknesse,
And bring their quaking flesh vnto the hooke:
The rout, they follow with confused voyce,
Crying, they'are glad, say they could ne're abide him;
Enquire, what man he was? what kind of face?
What beard he had? What nose? what lips? protest,
They euer did presage h' would come to this:
They never thought him wise, nor valiant: aske
After his garments, when he dies? what death?
And not a beast of all the herd demands,
What was his crime? or, who were his accusers?
Vnder what proofe, or testimonie, he fell?
There came (sayes one) a huge, long, worded letter
From *Capreae* against him. Did there so?
O, they are satisfied, no more . . .

Lepidus breaks in again:

                         . . . Alas!
They follow fortune, and hate men condemn'd,
Guiltie, or not. . . .

Arruntius, Jonson's spokesman, points the moral

          . . . But, had SEIANVS thriu'd
In his designe, and prosperously opprest
The old TIBERIVS, then, in that same minute,
These very raskals, that now rage like *furies*
Would haue proclaim'd SEIANVS emperour.   [5.766-804]

As one critic has remarked, "There is an attractive freshness about this. . . . But it represents only the *surface* of Juvenal. It is an abstraction from the text. What is absent is Juvenal's *wit*."[2] Jonson's notion of classical decorum forbade the mention of frying pans and pisspots in a tragedy. Both Juvenal and Jonson express contempt for the populace, but treat it differently. Juvenal's mob pretends to be struck by Sejanus's ugliness, Jonson's wants to know how he looked.[3] I think Juvenal actually found the mob, pretending to hate Sejanus and calling him ugly, funny. Jonson is more snobbish. His crowd is composed of "raskals"—a "rout." (Also, unlike the members of Juvenal's mob, who behold the fallen statue of Sejanus, Jonson's mob sees the corpse itself, a device that may have been intended to make the mob appear more bloodthirsty.) Juvenal's contempt is not directed at the crowd, but at the political ambition that drove Sejanus. Jonson, who may seriously have intended *Sejanus* as a warning (like Shakespeare's *Coriolanus*) of the dangers of misrule and anarchy, despised popular appeal.[4] Juvenal, living under the Empire, had no worries on that score. As his famous passage on "bread and circuses" (which Jonson, significantly, ignored), brings out forcefully, the Roman populace had ceased to matter politically, either as an electorate or as a mob. Jonson's disdain for the mob echoes his estimate of what we would call a "mass audience." He took pride in basing his plays on the best classical authorities. He refused to give his audiences revenge tragedies with murders and ghosts, offering instead critically correct and historically accurate drama based on the principles laid down by the Renaissance humanists. But the audience did not appreciate Jonson's pains and the frigid *Sejanus* flopped.

[II]

Unfortunately, we have no extended passage in verse to show what Jonson could have done with Juvenal's comic effects. But no one who has read *Epicoene* (1609) could help but wish Jonson had attempted to modernize Juvenal's satires in the manner of the neoclassical Imitators. In act 2, scene 2, when Truewit, afraid of being disinherited, attempts to dissuade Morose from marrying, Jonson turns to the sixth satire of Juvenal, a traditional source of libels against women. Why marry? asks Juvenal. There are more attractive options.

certe sanus eras. uxorem, Postume, ducis?
dic, qua Tisiphone, quibus exagitare colubris?
ferre potes dominam salvis tot restibus ullam,
cum pateant altae caligantesque fenestrae,
cum tibi vicinum se praebeat Aemilius pons?   [28-32]

[Surely you used to be sane. Postumus, are you taking a wife? Say what fury, what snakes are driving you mad? Can you stand a wife when there are so many ropes available, when there are so many high windows gaping, when the Aemilian bridge is practically your next door neighbor?]

Notice how Jonson anticipates the neoclassicists, such as John Oldham, and provides precise locations in London for Juvenal's in Rome.

Mary, your friends doe wonder, sir, the *Thames* being so neer, wherein you may drowne so handsomely; or *London*-bridge, at a low fall, with a fine leape, to hurry you downe the streame; or, such a delicate steeple, i' the towne, as *Bow*, to vault from; or, a brauer height, as *Pauls;* or, if you affected to doe it neerer home, and a shorter way, an excellent garret windore, into the street; or, a beame, in the said garret, with this halter; [s.d. *He shows him a halter.*] which they haue sent, and desire, that you would sooner commit your graue head to this knot, then to the wed-lock nooze; or, take a little sublimate, and goe out of the world, like a rat; or a flie (as one said) with a straw i' your arse; any way, rather, then to follow this goblin *matrimony.* (2.2.20-32)

Like Juvenal, Jonson makes Truewit both witty and contemptu-ous of his audience.[5] But Jonson's formula differs a bit. Instead of relying on indirect suggestion—as in "ferre potes dominam salvis tot restibus ullam?"—in which it is up to the reader to infer that it is better to hang yourself than marry, Jonson is explicit. The comic effect is created by the incongruous modifiers that make suicide resemble an Olympic event: "drowne so handsomely," "with a fine leape," "such a delicate steeple . . . to vault from," "affected to doe it neerer home" (as if Morose were being finicky). Like Juvenal, Johnson builds up to a ridiculous conclusion, but where Juvenal, as usual, piles one hyperbole atop another (though too many critics assume that the final suggestion—if you cannot get along without a bedmate, get a boy, who will be less demanding sexually—is serious evidence of Juvenal's tastes), Jonson diminishes and degrades: "and go out of the world, like a rat, or a flie . . . with a straw i' your arse."

Truewit continues with about one hundred lines, a precis of the entire sixth satire. Often he compresses a fairly long passage in the original: "so she may kisse a page, or a smooth chinne, that has despaire of a beard" (113-14), for example, is based on Juvenal's detailed account of how women delight in eunuchs who can, as distinguished from those who cannot, perform sexually (366-77). But when he uses particular examples, they are usually on the same scale as Juvenal's, such as the woman who loves to discuss politics or criticize literature.

haec eadem novit quid toto fiat in orbe,
quid Seres, quid Thraces agant . . .
   illa tamen gravior, quae cum discumbere coepit
laudat Vergilium, periturae ignoscit Elissae,
committit vates et comparet, inde Maronem
atque alia parte in trutina suspendit Homerum.   [434-37]

[She herself knows what is happening in the whole world, what the Chinese and the Thracians are up to. . . . What's worse, when she reclines at table she praises Virgil, forgives Dido about to perish, sets the poets against each other and weighs them, puts Virgil on one side of the scale, Homer on the other.]

. . . bee a states-woman, know all the newes, what was done at *Salisbury*, what at the *Bath*, what at court, what in progresse; or so shee may censure *poets*, and authors, and stiles, and compare 'hem, DANIEL with SPENSER, IONSON with the other youth, and so foorth. . . . (114-18)

Truewit's speech is tantalizing. Clearly Jonson could have created a version of a Roman satire that would have paralleled its original point for point with contemporary English examples. Unfortunately, it seems never to have occurred to Jonson that the form we call the Imitation was worth trying.

[III]

We might think of the adaptations from Horace that are incorporated into Jonson's comedy *Poetaster* (1601) as Imitations in reverse. Instead of adapting a Roman original to English circumstances, Jonson disguised a current quarrel—an affair known as the War of the Theatres, since it involved the rivalry between the private boys' company for whom Jonson wrote, the Children of the Chapel Royal, and the professional adult companies, including Shakespeare's—and set it in ancient Rome. The main targets of Jonson's satiric comedy were the playwrights Thomas Dekker and John Marston. Dekker appears as the imbecilic Demetrius Fannius (a conflation of two of Horace's favorite butts, see *Satires* 1.4.21, and 1.10.79-80), and Marston as the bumptious Crispinus (whose name is taken from the popular Stoic philosopher and versifier [*Sat.* 1.1.120-21] whose janitor converts Horace's servant Davus to Stoicism [2.7.45]). Jonson, never a man much troubled by false modesty, is Q. Horatius Flaccus himself.

    Poetaster has two direct borrowings from Horace. Act 3, scenes 1, 2, and 3, are based on the ninth satire of the first book, Horace's encounter with the impertinent bore who will not go away. Act 3, scene 5 (added in 1616) is a straightforward verse translation of the first satire of the second book, the dialogue with the lawyer Trebatius, in which Horace defends the nobility of the satirist's role.

    Unlike Horace's bore, who is anonymous, Jonson's is Crispinus himself, who declares that he is both a poet and a philosopher (3.1.23-28), recites his own verses, and comments on them. (Horace's bore spares us any samples.)

CRIS. *Rich was thy hap, sweet, deintie cap,*
      There to be placed:

> *Where thy smooth blacke, sleeke white may smacke,*
> *And both be graced.*
> *White,* is there vsurpt for her brow; her forehead: and then
> *sleeke,* as the *paralell* to *smooth,* that went before. A kind of
> *Paranomasie,* or *Agnomination:* doe you conceiue, sir?
> (85-91).

Just as today the literary-critical bore must be well supplied with
jargon, in the Renaissance a catalogue of rhetorical figures was
indispensable.

The Horatian *sermo,* itself dramatic, differs from dramatic
comedy in that the dramatist cannot leave his characters' actions
to the imagination of the audience, but must cue actors as to what
to say and do. In the original, Horace slips back and forth between
three different voices. The first one is Horace the narrator, who
relates the story, summarizes, and comments. Then we have the
interior monologue Horace delivers as he thrashes vainly in the
toils of the bore. And finally we have direct quotations from the
conversation between the bore and Horace. At first Horace tries
to get rid of the bore by pretending to be on his way to visit a
friend who is ill—nobody the bore knows, of course—who lives
far away across the Tiber. "That's all right," the bore replies, "I've
nothing better to do." Horace tries to scare him off by insinuating
his friend has the plague. Does the bore have any relatives who
might be sorry to lose him?

interpellandi locus hic erat "est tibi mater,
cognati, quis te salvo est opus?" "haud mihi quisquam.
omnis composui" "felices. nunc ego resto.
confice; namque instat fatum mihi triste, Sabella
quod puero cecinit divina mota anus urna:
'hunc neque dira venena nec hosticus auferet ensis
nec laterum dolor aut tussis nec tarda podagra:
garrulus hunc quando consumet cumque: loquaces,
si sapiat, vitet, simul atque adoleverit aetas.' "   [26-35]

[Here was my chance to interrupt. "Do you have a mother, relatives,
somebody who wants you to stay healthy?" "None at all, I've buried the

lot." "Lucky for them! Now it's my turn; get on with it; now the sad fate has arrived, which an old Sabellan woman, shaking her urn, prophesied for me as a boy: 'This fellow will not be killed by deadly poison, or an enemy sword, or pleurisy, or the cough, or the slow gout; at some time or other a non-stop talker will be the death of him; if he is wise, he will avoid blabbermouths, or that will finish him.' "]

First we hear the narrator, then the bore, then Horace (the character in the poem) cursing the bore under his breath and then quoting, in a mock-heroic oracular style that I have not tried to render, the witch's prediction of illocutionary demise. It is easy to imagine Horace the poet reading the satire aloud to his friends in the circle of Maecenas, changing his voice and expression to bring out each different speaker, like Chaucer reading the *Canterbury Tales* to his patrons. But Jonson, unfortunately, had to convert Horace's witty monologue into dialogue actors could recite, which meant that the character Horace has to speak his inner thoughts aloud, but without the bore's understanding what is bothering him.

> HORA. Is you mother liuing, sir?
> CRIS. Au: Conuert thy thoughts to somewhat else, I pray thee.
> HORA. You haue much of the mother in you, sir: your father is dead?
> CRIS. I, I, thanke IOVE, and my grand-father too, and all my kins-folkes, and well compos'd in their vrnes.
> HORA. The more their happinesse; that rest in peace,
> Free from th'abundant torture of thy tongue;
> Would I were with them too. CRIS. What's that, HORACE?
> HORA. I now remember me, sir, of a sad fate
> A cunning woman, one SABELLA sung,
> When in her vrne, she cast my destinie,
> I being but a child. CRIS. What was't, I pray thee?
> HORA. Shee told me, I should surely neuer perish
> By famine, poyson, or the enemies sword;
> The *hecticke* feuer, cough, or pleurisie,
> Should neuer hurt me; nor the tardie gowt:
> But in my time, I should be once surpriz'd,
> By a strong tedious talker, that should vexe

And almost bring me to consumption.
Therefore (if I were wise) she warn'd me shunne
All such long-winded monsters, as my bane:
For if I could but scape that one discourser,
I might (no doubt) proue an olde aged man.
By your leaue, sir?
    CRIS. Tut, tut: abandon this idle humour, 'tis nothing but
melancholy. . . . (182-209)

Latin students today are usually warned not to translate using
English cognates (an admonition I shall observe generally, but not
minutely, in my translations), but Jonson seems to have found
them a stimulus for his dialogue. The bore's "composui" becomes
Crispinus' "well-compos'd" and Horace's "resto" inspires "rest in
peace"; "Sabella" Jonson apparently took for a proper name. It is
hard to decide how much of the original he expected to show
through, but as the boys' theatres played to educated upper-class
audiences, some of the spectators should have enjoyed the turns
Jonson gave Horace.[6] One insult Jonson's Horace delivers, "You
haue much of the mother in you," is a pun that works only in
English. In Jonson's time "the mother" was what we call "hysteria" (a term derived from the Greek word for womb.)

    How did Jonson expect Horace to speak his inner monologue
aloud on stage? He cannot be using the familiar device of the aside,
because Crispinus interrupts him, asking "what's that HORACE?"
If Horace is supposed to be mumbling *sotto voce*, how can we hear
him if Crispinus cannot? Obviously Crispinus hears Horace
recount the old woman's prophecy, though he misses the application to himself. I am not sure how these three scenes would
play—revivals of *Poetaster* are not everyday occurrences—but
they do not read well. That Crispinus, eager to get into the literary
circle of Maecenas, would swallow a few insults is not hard to
believe, but having Horace continuously revile him for the 285
lines of scene 1 and the 29 lines of scene 2, where Horace begs his
friend Aristius Fuscus for relief, relief that the witty Fuscus
refuses, forfeits our sympathy. In the original we hear Horace
trying to be polite to the bore while groaning within from

exasperation. Instead of the original urbane and long-suffering
Horace, Jonson gives us the Renaissance satirist as we find him
in Donne and John Marston, the hairy-flanked descendant of a
satyr with a snook pretty well cocked.[7]

In the case of Jonson's other adaptation from Horace in
Poetaster, we do not have to wonder what an audience hearing it
in the theatre would catch. Jonson thought that his plays were real
works of literature and published them as his *Works*. In his
collected edition of 1616 he added a scene (act 3, scene 5) translated
directly from Horace's first satire of the second book, the dialogue
between Horace and the lawyer Trebatius on the propriety of
writing satire. As Alexander Pope was to discover later, the first
satire of the second book is the natural choice for any satirist who
wants to defend against a charge of malicious libel. It is a
"programmatic satire," in which the satirist upholds the legiti-
macy of his role. Horace began by recounting some readers'
responses to his first book of satires, and asks Trebatius to advise
him.

"Sunt quibus in satira videor nimis acer et ultra
legem tendere opus; sine nervis altera quidquid
composui pares esse putat similisque meorum
mille die versus deduci posse. Trebati,
quid faciam? praescribe." "quiescas." "ne faciam, inquis,
omnio versus?" "aio." "peream male, si non
optimum erat; verum nequeo dormire." "ter uncti
transnanto Tiberim, somno quibus est opus alto,
irriguumque mero sub noctem corpus habento.
aut si tantus amor scribendi te rapit, aude
Caesaris invicti res dicere, multa laborum
praemia laturus." "cupidum, pater optime, vires
deficiunt; neque enim quivis horrentia pilis
agmina nec fracta pereuntis cuspide Gallos
aut labentis equo describat volnera Parthi."

[*Horace:* To some I seem to be too bitter in my satires and to press the
work beyond the law; another party thinks whatever I've written as
without force, and that they could turn out a thousand verses a day like

mine. Tell me, Trebatius, what ought I do? *Trebatius:* Be silent. *Hor.* I'm
not, you say, to write any more verses? *Treb.* Right. *Hor.* Let me die, if
that's the best course. Truly, I cannot sleep. *Treb.* After oiling yourself,
swim across the Tiber three times (advice which would leave Horace
on the wrong side of the river) if you want to sleep soundly, and have
your body well soaked in wine in the evening, or, if the love of writing
seizes you, dare to celebrate the deeds of unconquered Caesar—you'll
likely receive great rewards. *Hor.* I wish I could, but I lack the ability;
not everyone, indeed, can write of battle lines horrid with spears and
Gauls fleeing with broken lances and the wounds of a Parthian falling
from his horse.]

Although Jonson translates closely, he needs two-thirds again
as many lines to render the passage.

There are, to whom I seeme excessiue sower;
And past a *satyres* law t'extend my power:
Others, that thinke what euer I haue writ
Wants pith, and matter to eternise it;
And that they could, in one daies light, disclose
A thousand verses, such as I compose.
What shall I doe, TREBATIVS? say. TREB. Surcease.
   HORA. And shall my *Muse* admit no more encrease?
   TREB. So I aduise. HORA. An ill death let mee die,
If 'twere not best; but sleep auoids mine eye:
And I vse these, lest nights should tedious seeme.
   TREB. Rather, contend to sleepe, and liue like them,
That holding golden sleepe in speciall price,
Rub'd with sweet oiles, swim siluer *Tyber* thrice,
And euery eu'en, with neat wine steeped be:
Or, if such loue of writing rauish thee,
Then dare to sing vnconquer'd CAESARS deeds;
Who cheeres such actions with abundant meeds.
   HORA. That, father, I desire; but when I trie,
I feele defects in euery facultie:
Nor is't a labour fit for euery pen,
To paint the horid troups of armed men;
The launces burst, in GALLIA's slaughtred forces;
Or wounded *Parthians*, tumbled from their horses.

Jonson has long been regarded as the literary grandfather of Dryden, Pope, and the English Augustans, and crude as the couplets are, they are a good start. Jonson avoids those two worst traps for the literal translator, obscure allusions and a tortured Latinate syntax. A few elements make the reader pause; the antecedent of "these" (11) must be "verses" although the real subject is *writing satire*, and the modern reader is likely to take "who cheers such actions" as referring to the poet applauding Caesar's deeds rather than to Caesar and his rewards to the poet. The Elizabethans, of course, had no "cheers" or "cheerleaders." The most striking primitive features occur in Jonson's departures from the original: "in one daies light, disclose" for "die ... deduce" is a flat-footed attempt to set up the rhyme word "compose" as well as to preserve Horace's *d* alliteration. Equally clumsy is Trebatius' "Surcease" and Horace's "And shall my *Muse* admit no more encrease." The flowery epithets may look backward to the Elizabethan "golden style" (as C. S. Lewis called it) or forward to the poetic diction of the Augustans, but expressions such as "golden sleepe," "sweet oiles," and "siluer *Tyber*" are inappropriate to the pedestrian style of Horatian satire, especially in the mouth of the laconic Trebatius. Poetic diction is necessary, though, when Horace denies that he can rise to the sublime heights epic poetry demands, a disclaimer itself phrased in superb epic diction. (In his taste for this kind of delicious foolishness Horace most resembles Chaucer, as, for instance, in the Franklin's Tale, where he solemnly assures us, "I ne kan no termes of astrologye," and follows with some twenty lines of astrological technicalities.) Here Jonson seems to be too low-keyed, though it is difficult to be certain. Possibly "horid" was then a Latinism, and "Gallia" must have been pompous even then. But surely "tumbled" sounded as low to Jonson's first readers as it does to us.[8]

At the end of the satire (and scene), Jonson takes a detour that leads, in a sense, into the eighteenth century. Horace ended with a pun that brings even the cautious and unimaginative Trebatius over to his side. Trebatius had warned:

"sed tamen ut monitus caveas, ne forte negoti
incutiat tibi quid sanctarum inscitia legum:
si mala condiderit in quem quis carmina, ius est
iudiciumque.". . .   [80-83]

["But so that warned you may be on guard, lest through ignorance of the
sacred laws you get into trouble: *Whosoever shall invent an evil song
against another, for him there is a law and a judgment.*"]

He is quoting the ancient Roman code of the Twelve Tables,
where "mala carmina" probably does not mean *lampoons*, but
spells (our word *charm* comes from this sense of *carmen*). Horace,
however, cleverly misses the point.

. . . "esto, siquis mala; sed bona siquis
iudice conderit laudatus Caesare? siquis
opprobriis dignum latraverit, integer ipse?"   [84-86]

["So be it, if they're *bad;* but suppose a praiseworthy poet creates poems
that are good in Caesar's opinion? If he satirizes (literally, barks at)
someone who deserves reproach, while honest himself?"]

He takes "mala" not as *evil* but as *inartistic* or *incompetent*, and also
makes a pun with "iudice," which means both a judge in the legal
sense and also a literary critic. Trebatius, like most straightmen,
is a trifle dense, and catches only the legal sense: "solventur risu
tabulae, tu missus abibis" (the case will be laughed out of court
and you will be discharged, 86).

The ending of this little dialogue reveals why Horace—however much we love his charm, wit, and essential sanity—
is no model for the serious hard-charging satirist. Horace strikes
safe targets ("opprobriis dignum") and makes sure that his satires
are inoffensive to the party in power ("iudice . . . Caesare").

Jonson's Horace makes an important qualification:

TREB. No, HORACE, I of force must yeeld to thee;
Only, take heed, as being aduis'd by mee,
Lest thou incurre some danger: Better pause,
Then rue thy ignorance of the sacred lawes;

There's iustice, and a great action may be su'd
'Gainst such, as wrong mens fames with verses lewd.
   HORA. I, with lewd verses; such as libels bee,
And aym'd at persons of good qualitie,
I reuerence and adore that iust decree:
But I they shall be sharp, yet modest rimes
That spare mens persons, and but taxe their crimes,
Such, shall in open court, find currant passe;
Were CAESAR iudge, and with the makers grace.
   TREB. Nay I'le adde more; if thou thy selfe being cleare,
Shalt taxe in person a man, fit to beare
Shame, and reproach, his sute shall quickly bee
Dissolu'd in laughter, and thou thence set free.   [124-40]

Despite his own outspokenness (he once nearly had his nose slit for sedition), Jonson depicts himself as following Horace in avoiding "libels . . . aym'd at persons of good qualitie." (Did he, by the way, mean of good *moral* or *social* quality? I doubt that he ever asked himself. Probably he meant both.) Yet Horace never promised to "spare mens persons, and but taxe their crimes"; Horace loved to torment particular persons so long as they could not hit back at a satirist enjoying political favor. Rather Jonson foreshadows what was to become, in the late seventeenth and early eighteenth centuries, the satirist's standard defense, required, I think, to square the role of the satirist with official morality, the Christian doctrine that we are to love our enemies. (Only a few years before, in 1599, the Archbishop of Canterbury had the satires of Marston burned.) The solution (at least in theory) was to hate the sin while continuing to love the sinner, by not identifying him as any specific person. In Swift's words:

Yet, Malice never was his Aim;
He lash'd the Vice, but spar'd the Name;
No Individual could resent,
Where Thousands equally were meant.

It is important to remember that much of the satirist's Christian pose was blague. "Verses on the Death of Dr. Swift" (from which the quotation comes) attacks a good number of Swift's enemies by name. And Jonson obviously expected us to recognize his enemies Marston and Dekker in *Poetaster*. How ill the role of general satirist fits even an Horatian persona comes out in Trebatius' reply, that it is all right to "taxe *in person* [my emphasis] a man, fit to beare / Shame, and reproach." But however threadbare the cloak of disinterested moralist, satirists were to continue to wear it for over a century—Pope cast it aside only in his last years.[9]

But the ending is Jonson's only innovation. Unlike the Augustans, Jonson was essentially an antiquary who wanted his ancients to be historically correct.[10] Rather than imagining what a Roman satirist would say were he alive in seventeenth-century England, Jonson tried to imagine seventeenth-century Englishmen as ancient Romans, an equally demanding task, though not one that has endeared Jonson to twentieth-century critics.[11] Jonson's classicism was not of the kind likely to encourage departures and adaptations of the Roman satirists. Only *Epicoene*, with its contemporary English setting, gives some idea of what Jonson could have accomplished had he been willing to jettison his critical principles. Jonson probably thought he was doing his readers a favor by giving them what they ought to like.

Early Seventeenth-Century Translators

[I]

Without thinking much about the matter, we tend to expect that the earliest translations of a work will be literal, and that freer versions will start to appear only after the demand for close translations has been satisfied. But the first published seventeenth-century version of the tenth satire of Juvenal is without doubt the strangest ever to see print. It is *That Which Seemes Best is Worst. Exprest in a Paraphrastical Transcript of Iuuenals Tenth Satyre. Together with the Tragicall Narration of Virginias Death Interserted*, by W[illiam] B[arksted?] (1617).[1] On the title page Barksted quotes the familiar advice from Horace's *Ars poetica:* "nec verbum verbo curabit reddere fidus / interpres" (the faithful interpreter will not care to reproduce word for word, 133)—a good luck charm often recited by translators about to take silly chances,[2] whether the famous schoolboy about to guess at the meaning of *oves* and to make Livy report that in early Rome the senators laid their own eggs, or a modern about to turn Euripides' *Bacchae* into a 1960s acid-rock musical. In the epigraph Barksted turns once again to the *Ars poetica*, quoting those famous remarks on poetic licence: ". . . pictoribus atque poetis / quidlibet audendi semper fuit aequa potestas. / veniam petimusque damusque vicissim" (Poets and painters always enjoyed an equal right to attempt whatever they liked. We seek and grant this indulgence in turn, 9-10). Barksted needed all the indulgence he could get.

On the title page, Barksted makes yet another attempt to appease the critical reader, with a couplet of his own composition.

The pith is *Iuuenals*, but not the rime:
All that is good is his, the rest is mine.

How much is "the rest"? There are 366 hexameter verses in the
tenth satire; Barksted's poem runs to 1,330 pentameter lines
arranged in couplets, of which 532 are Barksted's interpolated
poem on Appius and Virginia. But numbers do not tell the story.
Barksted becomes wordier and wordier as he pushes his way
further into the tenth satire. He treats Juvenal's famous opening
very literally.

Omnibus in terris, quae sunt a Gadibus usque
Auroram et Gangen, pauci dinoscere possunt
vera bona atque illis multum diversa, remota
erroris nebula. quid enim ratione timemus
aut cupimus? . . .

[In all the lands from Cadiz to Aurora and the Ganges, there are few able
to discern things truly good from those very much different, with the
cloud of error removed. What indeed do we fear or desire with reason?]

In all the lands, from *Gades* vnto the East
To *Ganges*, few there are who know what's best,
Or worst, though error's mist were quite remoued;
For what with reason is there feard or loued?

By the time Barksted reaches Juvenal's description of the
sorrows of a long life, he requires nearly twice as many lines as
Juvenal does verses. When Juvenal, never afraid to turn to
mythical examples when real ones are lacking, wants an example
of a very long life, he chooses Priam, the king of Troy in the *Iliad*.
Had he died while Troy still stood, the town would never have
seen a costlier funeral.

incolumi Troia Priamus venisset ad umbras
Assaraci magnis sollemnibus, Hectore funus

portante ac reliquis fratrum cervicibus inter
Iliadum lacrimas, ut primos edere planctus
Cassandra inciperet scissaque Polyxena palla,
si foret extinctus diverso tempore, quo non
coeperat audaces Paris aedificare carinas.
longa dies igitur quid contulit? omnia vidit
eversa et flammis Asiam ferroque cadentem.
tunc miles tremulus posita tulit arma tiara
et ruit ante aram summi Iovis ut vetulus bos,
qui domini cultris tenue et miserabile collum
praebet ab ingrato iam fastiditus aratro.
exitus ille utcumque hominis, sed torva canino
latravit rictu quae post hunc vixerat uxor.   [258-72]

[While Troy was still safe, Priam would have come to the shades of
Assaracus with a magnificent funeral, while Hector and the rest of his
brothers bore the coffin on their necks (Priam had fifty sons; surely
Juvenal is imagining a very long coffin) amidst the tears of Trojan
women, while Cassandra began to pour out lamentations and Polyxena
to rend her garments, had he died earlier, before Paris started building
his bold ships. What did length of days bring? He sees everything
overthrown and Asia falling to fire and sword. Then, a trembling
soldier, he put off his tiara and seized arms and before the altar of highest
Jupiter he fell like an old ox, a reject from the ungrateful plow, who
offers a skinny and miserable neck to the knife of his master. At least his
was the death of a man. His ugly old wife survived him barking with
a canine grimace.]

Barksted's verbose translation proves that more indeed can be less.

Had *Priam* died before the siege of *Troy*,
He might haue met *Assaracus* with ioy,
With great solemnitie and festiuals,
His children had performed his funerals,
And *Hector* and his brethren had him borne
Vnto his graue, while all the people mourne!
Cassandra had gone weeping all before,
And then *Polyxena* with garments tore.
O had he died before that *Paris* went
To build those ships which he for *Helen* sent!

Though this vntimely death might him displease,
Yet had he gone into his graue with peace;
Then had he died, he should but once haue died,
(In length of daies, alas! what good is spied?)
But liuing longer, woe is me therefore!
He liues to die ten thousand deaths and more:
He liues to see all spoil'd and ouerturned,
Asia with fire and sword consum'd and burned,
When like a souldier which with feare doth quake,
He layes aside his Crowne, and Armes doth take,
He flies, and on great Iupiter he calles,
And downe before his altars dead he falles,
Euen as an Oxe with age and toile quite done
Vnder the yoke for wearinesse doth grone:
So aged *Priam* ouercharg'd with woe,
Fainted and fell and could no farther goe:
And *Hecuba* his wife, which did suruiue,
Till she was turned into a dogge, did liue.   [B3v-B4r]

Barksted misses the contrast Juvenal creates by using epic diction,
phrases such as "coeperat audaces Paris aedificare carinas" and
"eversa et flammis Asiam ferroque cadentem," mingled with the
degrading comparison of Priam to a worn-out old ox, "vetulus
bos," about to have its throat cut and the allusion to Hecuba's
transformation into a barking bitch. Instead Barksted reflects that
for Priam an untimely death "might him displease" but would
have saved him "ten thousand deaths and more" (the "woe is me
therefore!" to set up the rhyme is especially clumsy). It also takes
Barksted a long time to despatch Priam. The passage reads as
though Barksted had never read the second book of the *Aeneid* and
did not know that Priam was slain by Achilles' son Neoptolemus.
Barksted makes it sound as if Priam had dropped dead of the strain
of carrying round all that armor. At least Barksted did not try to
expatiate on what happened to Hecuba.

Fortunately, Barksted's interpolated poem on Appius and Virginia has no place in the history of translations of Roman satire,
so the reader will be spared any samples. It has been said that the
poem shows Barksted "might have produced a good script for

Bottom to present, if Theseus had rejected Pyramus and Thisbe."³
When he returns to Juvenal, Barksted becomes more long-
winded than ever, needing 260 lines for Juvenal's last 72 verses.
Juvenal's passing allusions to Hippolytus and Bellerophon gave
Barksted an excuse for telling their stories at length, and his
warning that too often we choose our spouses "animorum /
impulsu et caeca magnaque cupidine ducti" (drawn on by whim
and a great and blind passion) sends Barksted on a 50-line excursus
on the distinction between love (a rose, naturally) and lust
("garlick"—apparently English distrust for Mediterranean cook-
ery dates back further than most of us were aware). One is
reminded of the Middle Ages as Barksted practices *amplificatio*,
delighting in telling readers things they must already know.

One change, though, is significant. In the famous conclusion
to the tenth satire, Juvenal asks if there is anything we *should* pray
for, and answers his question.

Nil ergo optabunt homines? si consilium vis,
permittes ipsis expendere numinibus quid
conveniat nobis rebusque sit utile nostris.
nam pro iucundis aptissima quaeque dabunt di:
carior est illis homo quam sibi. . . .   [346-50]

[Should men then pray for nothing? If you want advice, you'll let the
gods themselves supply what is suitable for us and for our condition. For
instead of pleasing things the gods give us those most appropriate. A man
is dearer to the gods than he is to himself.]

This passage has long been a favorite of Christian readers, but
Barksted seems to have anticipated Samuel Johnson's *The Vanity
of Human Wishes* in making Juvenal a monotheist.

What then? shall therefore men for nothing craue?
Soft! if thou seeke and wouldst my counsell haue;
Doe thus: seeke to those heauenly powers aboue,
Leaue all to them, for sure they doe vs loue,
Let God see first, what doth agree with vs,
What shall be fit, and most commodious.

God doth not giue according to our wit
For pleasant things, he giues vs what most fit.
Deerer is man to him, than man can be
Vnto himselfe . . .   [D1v]

Perhaps the essential congruity Barksted perceived between Juvenal's sentiments and the Christian faith comes through in the very
literalness of Barksted's translation: "consilium"/"counsell"; "numinibus"/"heauenly powers": "conveniat"/"agree"; "utile"/"fit"; "aptissima"/"commodious"; "iucundis"/"pleasant"; "carior"/"deerer"—
only "di" had to be put into the singular to allude to God. When
an author as willing as Barksted to take liberties remains so faithful
to the Latin, he must have felt Juvenal's religious position was
sound.

Both as a representation of the tenth satire and as an original
poem (which contemporary orthodoxy insists every good translation should be)[4] *That Which Seemes Best* is indeed one of the
worst. But for a student of classical satire in English it is a valuable
specimen, one that suggests some unexpected conclusions. First,
although obviously acquainted with rhetorical techniques, Barksted's
expansions and interpolations show that he was unaware of or
uninterested in the structure of the original and felt at liberty to
amplify and interpolate at will. Could some of the subtle arrangements critics have found in more highly regarded Renaissance
poems be illusory too? Second, taking a bold approach to a famous
ancient poem did not begin in the Restoration and does not
indicate anything characteristically *modern. That Which Seemes
Best* is not an Imitation, but anyone who could perpetrate on the
tenth satire what Barksted did would not shrink from resetting it
in seventeenth-century England, had the thought occurred to
him. Finally, the opposition, or even contradiction, that some
critics detect between Christianity and Juvenal's Stoicism seems
to have been invisible to a translator whose commitment to
Christian morality is unmistakable. When we talk about "seventeenth-century values," or argue that all "Renaissance" or "Restoration" people shared some particular belief, we might first look
at what they actually said and did, and for this purpose Barksted
is as good a witness as far better poets.

[II]

Although even as bad a poet as Barksted has something to teach
us, it is a pleasure to come across a little-known poet whose work
is well-worth reading for its own sake. Such is the case with Sir
John Beaumont (1583-1627). A Catholic recusant, Beaumont
would be a good model for the ancestor of some admirable minor
character in the later works of Evelyn Waugh. His faith cost him
most of his estate and he retired from the literary world of
London—he was one of the "sons of Ben"—to his remaining
property in Leicestershire, where he continued to write poetry,
mostly in heroic couplets that are indistinguishable, except for
spelling, from respectable eighteenth-century work. His best
known poem is a historical epic called *Bosworth Field*, but given
the sacrifices he had made for his principles it is appropriate that
his translations should include the sixth satire of the second book
of Horace, the second satire of Persius, and the tenth satire of
Juvenal, poems that celebrate the pleasures of retirement and
obscurity and emphasize that whatever misfortunes life brings,
happiness should be sought where it can always be found, in
virtue.

The sixth satire of the second book of Horace—like his second
epode and Claudian's poem on the old man who lived near Verona
and never saw the sun set anywhere but in his neighbor's field
(both also translated by Beaumont)—has always been a favorite
poem for homebodies. Horace begins with a prayer to Mercury,
the god of luck.

Hoc erat in votis: modus agri non ita magnus,
hortus ubi et tecto vicinus iugis aquae fons
et paulum silvae super his foret. auctius atque
di melius fecere. bene est. nil amplius oro,
Maia nate, nisi ut propria haec mihi munera faxis.
si neque maiorem feci ratione mala rem
nec sum facturus vitio culpave minorem . . .

[This was my prayer: a bit of property, not particularly large, a garden
and a neighboring fountain of ever-flowing water, and a little wood

beyond. The gods did more and better. That's well. I pray for no more, offspring of Maia, if you will let me keep these gifts my own, and if I never made my estate greater by foul means or smaller by vice or folly.]

Beaumont opens:

This was my wish: no ample space of ground,
T'include my Garden with a mod'rate bound,
And neere my house a Fountaine never dry,
A Little Wood, which might my wants supply,
The gods have made me blest with larger store:
It is sufficient, I desire no more,
O sonne of *Maia*, but this grant alone,
That quiet use may make these gifts mine owne.
If I increase them by no lawlesse way,
Nor through my fault will cause them to decay.[5]

"Beaumont did not generally weave his individual couplets together into significant larger systems of verse,"[6] but here, with two phrases to help out the rhyme ("with moderate bound" and "which might my wants supply"), Beaumont has welded five couplets into a single period, a feat that many a later couplet poet might envy.

There is only a little to indicate that the Horace's feelings have become Beaumont's, but it is suggestive that we see Beaumont hoping that "quiet use will make these gifts my owne," if only he "increase them by no lawlesse way"—note the change from perfect to future tense. When Beaumont was convicted of recusancy the crown handed over two thirds of his property to Sir James Sempill, a Scotchman who wrote anti-Catholic verses,[7] and Beaumont must have had some painful reflections on what was "lawlesse" in the sight of man, and of God.

After Horace imagined himself shoved about and insulted by an urban crowd, then besieged by place-seekers and gossip-mongers eager to cash in on his friendship with Maecenas—a most unpolitical friendship, Horace assures us—he wishes he were at his ease in the country, free to delight in peace and leisure.

o rus, quando ego te aspiciam quandoque licebit
nunc veterum libris, nunc somno et inertibus horis
ducere sollicitae iucunda oblivia vitae?
o quando faba Pythagorae cognata simulque
uncta satis pingui ponentur holuscula lardo?
o noctes cenaeque deum, quibus ipse meique
ante Larem proprium vescor vernasque procaces
pasco libatis dapibus. prout cuique libido est,
siccat inaequalis calices conviva solutus
legibus insanis, seu quis capit acria fortis
pocula seu modicis uvescit laetius. ergo
sermo oritur, non de villis domibusve alienis,
nec male necne Lepos saltet; sed, quod magis ad nos
pertinet et nescire malum est, agitamus, utrumne
divitiis homines an sint virtute beati;
quidve ad amicitias, usus rectumne, trahat nos
et quae sit nature boni summumque quid eius.   [60-76]

[O country, when shall I see you again? When can I pass happy times free of the cares of life, with my favorite books, with sleep and leisurely hours. O when will Pythagoras' relative, the bean, be served along with "veggies" oiled with a lot of lard? O nights and meals of the gods, when I feed myself and my insolent servants before my own household gods. Each guest may drain unequal cups in proportion to his thirst, released from silly rules, whether he takes a strong draft or is happily refreshed with a moderate amount. Then conversation begins, not about villas and real estate, or whether Lepos dances badly or not, but about things more important to us that it would be wrong not to know: whether men are made happy by riches or by virtue; whether expediency or principle draws us into friendship, and what is the nature and highest kind of the good.]

This is a standard satiric topos—not necessarily a description of real life on Horace's Sabine farm or anywhere else. Horace thinks of spending his time reading Greek poetry, undisturbed by the cares of the world—to which he is largely a spectator anyway—dining simply and wholesomely on home-grown vegetables, and discussing philosophic questions with a few intimate friends.

Like later close translators, Beaumont leaves what was obscure in his original obscure in translation.

> ... when shall my sight
> Againe bee happy in beholding thee
> My countrey farme? or when shall I be free
> To reade in bookes what ancient writers speake,
> To rest in sleepe, which others may not breake,
> To taste (in houres secure from courtly strife)
> The soft oblivion of a carefull life?
> O when shall beanes upon my boord appeare,
> Which wise *Pythagoras* esteem'd so deare?
> Or when shall fatnesse of the Lard anoint
> The herbes, which for my table I appoint?
> O suppers of the Gods! O nights divine!
> When I before our Lar might feast with mine,
> And feed my prating slaves with tasted meate,
> As ev'ry one should have desire to eate.
> The frolicke guest not bound with heavy lawes,
> The liquor from unequall measures drawes:
> Some being strong delight in larger draughts,
> Some call for lesser cups to cleere their thoughts.
> Of others house and lands no speaches grow
> Nor whether *Lepos* danceth well or no.
> We talke of things which to our selves pertaine,
> Which not to know would be a sinfull staine.
> Are men by riches or be vertue blest?
> Of friendships ends is use or right the best?
> Of good what is the nature, what excells? [86-111]

The beans were dear to Pythagoras because he believed that souls were reincarnated, so that when one ate a bird, or even a bean, one might be eating one's "grandam."[8] Roman formal etiquette required a *magister bibendi* to decide whether the wine was to be strong or weak (the ancients normally watered their wine) and everyone had to submit to his decision. In Horace's idyllic informal setting everyone can please himself. The "Lar" and the slaves are appropriate only to Roman religion and society; like his master, Jonson, Beaumont maintains the antiquity of the piece. Yet Beaumont's verse is better than Jonson's. The careful blending of *f* and *l* in "soft oblivion of a careful life" could not be improved upon even by Alexander Pope. If anything Beaumont goes astray by not being pedestrian enough. "Or when shall fatnesse of the Lard anoint / The Herbes, which for my table I appoint," with its elaborate inversion and odd predication, as well as its alliterating rhyme—which I find obvious and jingly—seems too artificial for Horace's "uncta satis pingui ponentur holuscula lardo?" especially with its diminutives.[9]

Although Beaumont's editor calls the first satire of the second book "the most readable of all Beaumont's translations" (p. 236), I prefer the versions of the second satire of Persius and the tenth satire of Juvenal. His verse technique is just as good and—in the case of Juvenal at least—closer to the style of the original. Beaumont's love of moralizing (his original poems include "A Dialogue between the World, a Pilgrim, and Vertue," "An act of Contrition," and "Of the miserable state of Man") finds more scope than in Horace, and the literal mode of translation works better for poems that depend less on familiarity with Roman social customs, as they are concerned with moral truths, which are (it was believed in Beaumont's day) always and everywhere the same.

Persius' second satire treats the same subject as Juvenal's more famous tenth, praying for the wrong things. But Persius, as we should expect of a practicing Stoic, concerns himself more than Juvenal with the spiritual state of the suppliant, a hypocrite who prays loudly for "mens bona, fama, fides" ("a sound mind, good reputation, and trustworthiness"—Beaumont's "gifts of minde, fame, faith" strikes me as at once too literal and misleadingly Christian), while at the same time whispering his request that a rich uncle die suddenly, his plow strike buried treasure, or that the person ahead of him in line for an inheritance drop dead. Then, in one of those apostrophes satirists so enjoy, Persius turns to the worshipper and asks how he can tell Jupiter what he would be horrified to tell his best friend.

haec sancte ut poscas, Tiberino in gurgite mergis
mane caput bis terque et noctem flumine purgas.
heus age, responde (minimum est quod scire laboro)
de Iove quid sentis? estne ut praeponere cures

hunc—"cuinam?" cuinam? vis Staio? an scilicet haeres?
quid potior iudex, puerisve quis aptior orbis?
hoc igitur, quo tu Iovis aurem inpellere temptas,
dic agedum Staio: "pro Iuppiter, o bone" clamet
"Iuppiter!" at sese non clamet Iuppiter ipse?   [15-23]

[Do you stick your head three or four times in the whirling Tiber and
wash all night in the river so you can pray for things like these, holy one?
Come on, answer—I'd like to know this, at least—what do you think of
Jupiter? Is there someone you esteem more highly? "Who?" Who?
What about Staius? You're stuck? Who'd be a better judge? Who's fairer
to widows and orphans? Ask Staius to do what you've just asked of
Jupiter. "By Jove, my good man!" he'd shout, "By Jove!" And wouldn't
Jove himself exclaim, "By Jove!"]

Beaumont's enjambments break up the smooth flow of the couplets, to match the staccato rhythms of Persius' rapid-fire ques-
tion-and-answer style.

Those are the holy pray'rs for which thy head
(When first the morning hath her mantle spred)
Is dipt so many times in *Tibers* streames,
When running waters purge the nightly dreames.
I thus demand: in answer be not slow,
It is not much that I desire to know:
Of *Jove* what think'st thou? if thy judgement can
Esteeme him juster than a mortall man?
Then *Staius?* doubt'st thou which of these is best
To judge aright the fatherlesse opprest?
The speech with which thine impious wishes dare
Prophane *Joves* eares, to *Staius* now declare:
O *Jove*, O good *Jove*, he will straight exclaime,
And shall not *Jove* crie out on his owne name?   [23-36]

I miss most Persius' sense of humor as he builds toward the climax
of having Jupiter swear by Jupiter. (The "By Jove" repeated in
my crib attempts to preserve the joke, though with a flavor that
smacks more of Victoria's reign than of Nero's.)

As in the translation from Horace, here Beaumont does little to make references to Roman practices intelligible.[10] Persius is one of the most obscure of the Latin poets, much given to the sort of homely metaphors and allusions that in the Renaissance were called "dark conceits." It is from him that the Elizabethans got the idea that satirists should be incomprehensible to the uninitiated. Take for example the close of the second satire. Its moral, that the gods prefer simple offerings from the upright and pure of heart to vessels of gold from the degenerate and greedy, is an obvious commonplace of the kind Renaissance Christian stoics loved. But to make the point Persius mixes metaphors of adulterating oil, wool dyeing, and mining.

o curvae in terris animae et caelestius inanis!
quid iuvat hoc, templis nostros immittere mores
et bona dis ex hac scelerata ducere pulpa?
haec sibi corrupto casiam dissolvit olivo,
et Calabrum coxit vitiato murice vellus;
haec bacam conchae rasisse et stringere venas
ferventis massae crudo et pulvere iussit.
peccat et haec, peccat, vitio tamen utitur. at vos
dicite, pontifices: in sancto quid facit aurum?
nempe hoc quod Veneri donatae a virgine pupae.
quin damus id superis, de magna quod dare lance
non possit magni Messalae lippa propago:
compositum ius fasque animo sanctosque recessus
mentis et incoctum generoso pectus honesto.
haec cedo ut admoveam templis, et farre litabo.   [61-75]

[O souls bent to earth and empty of heavenly things! What good does this do, to bring our own habits into the temples and decide what to the gods is good from our own depraved flesh. This (that is, the flesh) to please itself dissolved cassia in adulterated olive oil, and boiled Calabrian wool in tainted purple dye; this bade us take the pearl from the shell and strip the veins of glowing ore from the raw dust. This sins and sins, and still enjoys vice. But tell us, you priests: what good is gold in the sanctuary? It's worth as much as dolls dedicated by a virgin to Venus. Let us offer instead what the bleary-eyed offspring of Messala cannot offer from a big platter; justice and rectitude fixed in the mind, a mind pure within, and a heart full of noble honesty. Let me approach the temple with these, and I'll worship with a little flour.]

In Beaumont's version:

O crooked soules, declining to the earth
Whose empty thoughts forget their heav'nly birth:
What end, what profit have we, when we strive
Our manners to the Temples to derive?
Can we suppose, that to the gods we bring
Some pleasing good from this corrupted Spring?
This flesh, which Casia doth dissolve and spoyle,
And with that mixture taints the native oyle:
This boyles the fish with purple liquor full,
And staines the whitenesse of Calabrian wooll.
This from the shell scrapes out the Pearle, and straines
From raw rude earth the fervent Metals veines,
This sinnes, it sinnes, yet makes some use of vice:
But tell me, ye great Flamins, can the price
Raise Gold to more account in holy things,
Than Babies, which the maide to *Venus* brings?
Nay rather let us yeeld the gods such gifts,
As great *Messallaes* off-spring never lifts,
In costly Chargers stretcht to ample space,
Because degen'rate from his noble race:
A soule, where just, and pious thoughts are chain'd;
A mind, whose secret corners are unstain'd:
A brest, in which all gen'rous vertues lie,
And paint it with a never-fading die.
Thus to the Temples let me come with zeale,
The gods will heare me, though I offer meale.   [89-114]

Beaumont introduces some paraphrases, perhaps to make his meaning clearer, or to fill out the second line of the couplet. Considering the opaque translation, I think the latter more likely. At first glance one might assume that the cassia was dissolving the flesh and mixing it with the oil; comparison with the Latin shows that "which" is the subject in line 95 and "casia" the direct object. The "fish with purple liquor full" is not one of the scaly breed, but a shellfish called the *murex*, which abounded in the harbor of ancient Tyre and from which was extracted a costly dye known as "Tyrian purple"—at least Beaumont's original audience would have known that "purple" was actually the color we call red. The point is that Calabrian wool is of very high quality, so that treatment with expensive dye was a useless luxury, especially because the toga—the most elaborate garment an ordinary Roman would wear—donned on formal occasions only (and we know from Juvenal that having to wear one was regarded as a nuisance) is white. I suppose that Beaumont picked the pompous "Flamins" to translate "pontifices" because he needed a disyllable for "priests" (his Roman Catholicism may have put him off "pontiffs"). "Babies"—as Beaumont's editor noted—are actually dolls (Latin *pupa* gives us *poppet*) not infants, but the point escapes us unless we know that Roman girls left their dolls in the temple of Venus on reaching marriageable age.[11] Specific details and allusions get short shrift, while moral sentiments are elaborated. Notice how verses 71-74 of Persius expand to lines 105-12 of Beaumont's version. In apposition to "gifts" Beaumont gives us "A soule," "A mind," and "A brest," all composing the first foot and following caesura. The parallel structure emphasizes their essential similarity.

[III]

Beaumont's style is like his life, graceful but self-effacing, and quite adequate for Horace and Persius, who regarded satire as versified talk. But what did Beaumont make of the elevated style of Juvenal?[12] The sublime style is marked by an especial fondness for paraphrasis, for substituting poetic diction for terms of ordinary speech, for avoiding metrical effects that would have sounded cacophonous to the Roman ear, and for arranging carefully individual verses into longer periods. Typical is Juvenal's warning that answered prayers can have drastic results. It begins with a *sententia*, which runs into the following verse to maintain the flow of the passage. The rest of the verse and the succeeding six, forming one period, enumerate particular desires: civil power, military, eloquence, physical strength, and, especially, wealth.

evertere domos totas optantibus ipsis
di faciles. nocitura toga, nocitura petuntur
militia; torrens dicendi copia multis
et sua mortifera est facundia, viribus ille
confisus periit admirandisque lacertis,
sed plures nimia congesta pecunia cura
strangulat et cuncta exuperans patrimonia census
quanto delphinis balaena Britannica maior.   [7-14]

[The gods easily have overturned whole houses by fulfilling their owners' prayers. Dangerous civil power, dangerous military authority are sought; their own loquacity and eloquence are fatal to many; another was caught and killed by his strength and marvelous muscles; and even more have been choked by a great pile of money and wealth exceeding their patrimonies by as much as the British whale is bigger than the dolphin.]

Having opened the subject of the dangers of wealth, Juvenal pours on his examples, capped by two more *sententiae*.

temporibus diris igitur iussuque Neronis
Longinum et magnos Senecae praedivitis hortos
clausit et egregias Lateranorum obsidet aedes
tota cohors: rarus venit in cenacula miles.
pauca licet portes argenti vascula puri
nocte iter ingressus, gladium contumque timebis
et motae ad lunam trepidabis harundinis umbram:
cantabit vacuus coram latrone viator.   [15-22]

[In dire times and by order of Nero an entire cohort seized Longinus and the great gardens of rich Seneca and besieged the famous palaces of the Laterani: but a soldier only rarely comes into a garret. If you go out at night carrying even a few little dishes of pure silver, you will fear the sword and the club and the shadow of the reed in the moonlight: the empty-handed traveler can sing in the face of the robber.]

Again, watch how well Beaumont arranges his couplets into larger units.

The easie gods cause houses to decay,
By granting that, for which the owners pray;
In Peace and Warre we aske for hurtfull things,
The copious flood of speech to many brings
Untimely death; another rashly dyes,
While he upon his wondrous strength relyes:
But most by heapes of money choked are,
Which they have gather'd with too earnest care,
Till others they in wealth as much excell,
As British Whales above the Dolphins swell.   [9-18]

As in the original, the *sententia* is followed by a long period, which Beaumont extends through eight lines organized in two syntactic units each consisting of two couplets. The next passage is just as symmetrical.

In bloody times by *Neroes* fierce commands,
The armed troope about *Longinus* stands,
Rich *Senecaes* large gardens circling round,
And *Lateranus* Palace much renown'd.
The greedy Tyrants souldier seldome comes,
To ransack beggers in the upper roomes.
If silver vessels, though but few thou bear'st,
Thou in the night the sword and trunchion fear'st;
And at the shadow of each Reed wilt quake,
When by the Moone light thou perceiv'st it shake:
But he that travailes empty, feeles no griefe,
And boldly sings in presence of the thiefe.   [19-30]

Sell notes that Beaumont has expanded Juvenal's "rarus venit in cenacula miles" into a couplet, "ensuring that the point registers— whose the soldier is and whose the rooms are." Sell finds no such excuse for the last two couplets, which he calls "cumbersome, and less suggestive than Juvenal's brevity." I believe that Sell is correct and that Beaumont's trouble in equaling Juvenal's sharp thrusts comes not only from the fact that Latin is a much more compressed language than English, but from Beaumont's very smoothness. It remained for the next century to discover that a line with a strong caesura and parallel or chiastic hemistichs best echoes the thunderclap of one of Juvenal's *sententiae*.[13] Beaumont tends to avoid stops within the line, more often in Juvenal than in Horace or Persius. Perhaps he was trying to match the flow of Juvenal's periods by using the caesura sparingly.

Beaumont's expansions, whether prompted to inform the reader or by the need to fill up the couplet, sometimes get him into trouble. In the heroic couplet the second line is a particularly dangerous place for the unwary poet. Its rhyming word is the most emphatic in the couplet and a silly word, perhaps chosen simply to make the rhyme, will surely stand out. Beaumont never sinks to Barksted's level of idiocy, but he does slip at times. Someone who lived too long was King Nestor, says Juvenal: "rex Pylius, magno si quicquam credis Homero, / exemplum vitae fuit a cornice secundae" (The Pylian king, if you believe anything in great Homer, was an example of a life second only to a crow's, 246-47). Beaumont's version

The *Pylian* King, as Homers verses show,
In length of life came nearest to the Crow.　　　　　　　[337-38]

sounds namby-pamby, not contemptuous. The same happens a few lines later when Juvenal's cryptic "atque alius cui fas Ithacum lugere nantantem" (and the other whose fate it was to weep for the swimming Ithacan, 257) becomes

And sad *Laertes*, who had cause to weepe
For his *Ulisses* swimming on the deepe.　　　　　　　　[353-54]

It is not fair to compare Beaumont to the neoclassicists, who after all had the advantages of drawing on George Sandys, Sir John Denham, Sir Richard Fanshawe, and Edmund Waller. I doubt that Beaumont would care very much what we think of him as a technician. For him the most important facet of the Roman satirists was their morality. Before leaving Beaumont we should hear his version of Juvenal the moralist at his best.[14]

Shall men wish nothing? wilt thou counsell take,
Permit the heav'nly powers the choyce to make,
What shall be most convenient for our Fates,
Or bring most profit to our doubtfull states,
The prudent gods can place their gifts aright,
And grant true goods in stead of vaine delight.
A man is never to himselfe so deare,
As unto them when they his fortunes steare:
We carried with the fury of our minds,
And strong affection which our judgement blinds,
Would husbands prove, and fathers, but they see
What our wisht children and our wives will bee:
Yet that I may to thee some pray'rs allow,
When to the sacred Temples thou do'st vow,
Divinest entrailes in white Porkets found,
Pray for a sound mind in a body sound;
Desire brave spirit free from feare of death,
Which can esteeme the latest houre of breath,
Among the gifts of Nature, which can beare
All sorrowes from desire and anger cleare,
And thinkes the paines of *Hercules* more blest,
Then wanton lust the suppers and soft rest,
Wherein *Sardanapalus* joy'd to live.
I show thee what thou to thy selfe mayst give;
If thou the way to quiet life wilt treade,
No guide but vertue can thee thither leade:
No pow'r divine is ever absent there,
Where wisdome dwells, and equall rule doth beare.
But we, O Fortune, strive to make thee great,
Plac'd as a Goddesse in a heav'nly seate.   [489-518]

Today this idea is unfashionable, endorsing as it does quietism and
passivity. But Beaumont's religion left him no choice but to tread
"the way to quiet life"—let us hope he found it.

Barten Holyday's Juvenal and Persius

[I]

We could treat Barten Holyday almost anywhere in the first two-thirds of this study. His version of the satires of Persius appeared in 1616; it was to reappear, with the first publication of Holyday's translation of Juvenal, some sixty years later.[1] Although Holyday was a contemporary of Ben Jonson, who lent him a manuscript, his Juvenal belongs also to the world of John Dryden and Lord Rochester. From the little biographical material available, and the evidence presented by the volume itself, Holyday must have spent the years up till his death in 1661 adding to his commentary.[2] The result, a handsome piece of seventeeth-century book making decorated with many engravings, lets one imagine what would have happened if Dorothea had carried out Casaubon's last wishes, avoided Ladislaw, and devoted the rest of her life, *causa pietatis*, to preparing and seeing through the press an *edition deluxe* of *The Key to All Mythologies*.

Holyday "might, had he not acted the vain Man, been made a Bishop, or at least a Dean of a rich Church," wrote Anthony à Wood,[3] and his opinion is supported by Holyday's preface. The preface is an early example of something without which no scholarly book is complete, a page of acknowledgements ostensibly intended to thank other scholars for their help, but actually to show that the author knows all the right people.

My honour'd friend Mr. *John Selden* (of such eminency in the Studies of Antiquities and Languages) and Mr. *Farnaby* (whose learned Industry speaks so much for him in a little) procur'd me a fair Manuscript Copy

from the famous Library at Saint *James*'s, and a Manuscript Commentary
from our Herald of Learning, Mr. *Cambden*. My dear friend, the
Patriarch of our Poets, *Ben. Johnson* sent-in also an ancient Manuscript
partly written in the *Saxon* Character. My learned friend Dr. *Merick
Causabon* [*sic*] afforded likewise an elegant Manuscript from the Study
of his exact Father. (a2v)

John Selden and William Camden discovered, among other
things, medieval studies. Meric Casaubon was the son of the
famous classical scholar Isaac Casaubon. Both Meric Casaubon
and Holyday were students of Christ Church.

The best-known critical judgment ever delivered on Holyday's
translation is John Dryden's in the "Discourse Concerning the
Original and Progress of Satire," which precedes the 1692 transla-
tion of Juvenal and Persius. Dryden was particularly severe about
Holyday's attempt to turn each Latin hexameter into one line of
English.

Holiday, without considering that he Writ with the disavantage of Four
Syllables less in every Verse, endeavours to make one of his Lines, to
comprehend the Sense of one of *Juvenal*'s. According to the falsity of
the Proposition, was the Success. He was forc'd to crowd his Verse with
ill sounding Monosyllables, of which our Barbarous Language affords
him a wild plenty: And by that means he arriv'd at his Pedantick end,
which was to make a literal Translation: His Verses have nothing of
Verse in them, but only the worst part of it, the Rhyme: And that, into
the bargain, is far from good. But what is more Intollerable, by cram-
ming his ill chosen, and worse sounding Monosyllables so close together; the very Sense which he endeavours to explain is become more
obscure, than that of his Author. So that *Holiday* himself cannot be
understood, without as large a Commentary, than that which he makes
on [Juvenal and Persius].[4]

Actually, Dryden did not mind borrowing from Holyday when
he needed a rhyme. And unlike Dryden, who was arguing that a
translation should be as well written as a contemporary English
poem, we should judge Holyday by the standards of 1620, when
the work on Juvenal must have been under way, not by those of
1674, when it finally appeared. We could as reasonably compare

a Sopwith Camel to an F-16 Fighting Falcon as compare Holy-day's couplets to Dryden's.

In his preface Holyday said he was

studying to make my Translation first True, next as free from Annota-tions, as the Argument would permit. But the work implying such plenty of Antiquities, I had wronged both the Work and the Reader had I left them in darkness. (b1r)

If Holyday really was trying to control his itch to annotate, he was very unsuccessful. The first six satires have compact "Notes," but all sixteen are accompanied by "Illustrations"—rambling excur-suses on ancient life as well as commentary on the text, and containing huge mounds of information—and misinformation—inspired, for all one can tell, by free association. To sample a full-dress note of Holyday's—and not one of the longer ones—here is the comment on Juvenal's "Frontonis platani convulsaque marmora clamant / semper et adsiduo ruptae lectore columnae" (*Sat.* 1.12-13).

Fronto's Plane-trees. A noble *Roman* famous for learning and bounty, who used to lend his stately house encompassed with shady trees, to the Poets of his time, wherein they did read their Poems. This is at large describ'd by *Persius* in his first Satyre, and by *Juvenal* in his seventh. Of the delightful shade and spreading branches of the *Plane*-tree, see *Claudius Minos* on *Pliny, lib.* 1. *epist.* 3. *Bisciola* in his *Hor. Subseciv. lib.* 9. *cap.* 21. and *Wowerus de Umbra, cap.* 26. [There actually is such a book, Johannes Wower's *Dies Aestiva sive de umbra Paegnon* ("Summer day, or a Jeu d'esprit about Shade"), published in Hamburg in 1610 and reprinted in Oxford in 1636.] The imitation of this *Roman* custome of publique and Voluntary reading, though not in such a manner of place, hath been heretofore amongst Us; as Mr. *Camden* notes in his Epistle before his *Anglica, Normannica, &c.* For when *Giraldus Cambrensis* was return'd out of *Ireland* with *John*, King *Henry* the second's Son, to whom he was Tutour, he read publiquely in *Oxford*, in the year 1200, his Topographie of *Ireland.* (p. 11)

It is tempting to assume that Holyday was not trying to write serious scholarship, but emulating another student of Christ Church, doing for Juvenal what Robert Burton did for Melancholy. But anyone who has spent much time with scholars knows that the instinct to go for the capillaries is not peculiar to the seventeenth century. At least one aspect of Holyday's commentary ought to be investigated further, the illustrations. Most of the engravings were made by David Loggan, engraver for Oxford University, but where did he get his models? He must have derived his ideas about the appearance of ancient artifacts and his maps from somewhere, and in an age when archaeology was not even in its infancy, the only sources of knowledge of ancient life and art were illustrations in the margins of old manuscripts (if one was lucky), pseudoclassical Italian fakery, and a vivid imagination.[5] Most of the engravings are carefully matched to passages in the commentary. Did Holyday leave instructions concerning which passages to illustrate, and did he provide references to illustrations in other books to be copied? Did he even supply drawings of his own?

Despite Dryden's criticisms, Holyday usually translated into quite lucid English. But not when Juvenal depicts an orgy. In the sixth satire, Juvenal gives his version of what happened when women celebrated the rites of the Bona Dea, a religious ceremony from which men were barred.[6]

nota bonae secreta deae, cum tibia lumbos
incitat et cornu pariter vinoque feruntur
attonitae crinemque rotant ululantque Priapi
maenades. o quantus tunc illis mentibus ardor
concubitus, quae vox saltante libidine, quantus
ille meri veteris per crura madentia torrens!
lenonum ancillas posita Laufella corona
provocat et tollit pendentis praemia coxae,
ipsa Medullinae fluctum crisantis adorat:
palma inter dominas, virtus natalibus aequa.
nil ibi per ludum simulabitur, omnia fient
ad verum, quibus incendi iam frigidus aevo
Laomedontiades et Nestoris hirnea possit.
tunc prurigo morae inpatiens, tum femina simplex,
ac pariter toto repetitus clamor ab antro
"iam fas est, admitte viros." dormitat adulter,

illa iubet sumpto iuvenem properare cucullo;
si nihil est, servis incurritur; abstuleris spem
servorum, venit et conductus aquarius; hic si
quaeritur et desunt homines, mora nulla per ipsam
quo minus inposito clunem committat asello.   [314-34]

[The secrets of the Good Goddess are well known, when the flute excites the loins and the Maenads of Priapus carried away by the music and wine fling their hair about and scream. What craving for sex, what clamor of mounting desire, what a torrent of vintage wine pouring over their wet ankles! Challenging the slave girls belonging to brothel-keepers, Laufella wins the prize with her frenzied thighs, but she adores the juices that flow as Medullina comes: the ladies take the honors—their skill equals their social standing. Nothing is faked, everything's for real and would fire up frigid old King Priam and give Nestor an erection. Then their itch will brook no delay, they're totally female, as from every part of the hall the cry rebounds, "Now's the time to let in the men!" If her lover is sleeping, she orders a youth to throw on a robe and hurry; if none's available, the servants' quarters are invaded; remove any chance of servants and they'll hire the water carrier; if there are no men at all, straightway she'll offer her bottom to be mounted by a donkey.]

Modern readers who believe the sixth satire reflects what Juvenal really thought, impute to him a neurotic hatred of women and concoct psychological or biographical explanations.[7] Not so Holyday, who refers only to Juvenal's "overplus zeal of speech" and "plainness." Like some of the Church Fathers, Holyday may have believed that Juvenal faithfully described the "moral decay" that caused the fall of the Roman Empire and that aristocratic Roman matrons devoted their evenings to group sex. Whatever Holiday thought, he chose "to contract some things, and leave out some" (p. 117).

The Rites of the *Good Goddess* now to light
Are brought: where Pipe and Horn and Wine incite:
Where these astonish'd *Maenades* ne're shame,
To run with rowling hair. O inward flame!
The Leud *Lawfella* makes a Game of Sinne:
Rewards proposes, and rewards does winne.

Shee to worse *Medullina* yet gives place:
The Worse the Nobler! Thus they mount to grace!
Here's nothing feign'd; All's True: Enough to fire
Old *Priamus*, and *Nestor's* maim'd desire.
But when these very Women have all done,
Impatiently from these Deceits they run.
A Lover they 'll not want; though Some do blind
Nature's broad Light and Sin below their Kind!   [pp. 97-98]

Like some Victorian translators and commentators, Holyday
seems at pains to avoid bringing a blush to the cheek of a young
person and yet to make it clear that he is a sophisticated man of
the world who knows what Juvenal is talking about. "Sin below
their Kind" would mean little to anyone who could not read the
Latin original.

   Where Juvenal becomes prolix, Dryden's charge that Holyday
is obscure is sometimes justified. In the twelfth satire Juvenal
congratulates his friend Catullus on a narrow escape from ship-
wreck, and contrasts the modest offering he will make in thanks-
giving for his friend's safety with the extravagant sacrifices legacy-
hunters make for the health of their prospective testators—
hecatombs of oxen, and oxen only because elephants are unavail-
able. Then Juvenal launches a Shandyesque digression on the
history and habits of elephants.

   . . . existunt qui promittant hecatomben,
quatenus hic non sunt nec venales elephanti,
nec Latio aut usquam sub nostro sidere talis
belua concipitur, sed furva gente petita
arboribus Rutulis et Turni pascitur agro,
Caesaris armentum nulli servire paratum
privato, siquidem Tyrio parere solebant
Hannibali et nostris ducibus regique Molosso
horum maiores ac dorso ferre cohortis,
partem aliquam belli, et euntem in proelia turrem.   [101-10]

[There are some who promise a hecatomb, as there are no elephants for
sale here, nor is such a beast ever conceived in Latium or under our sky,

but sought in the land of the swarthy people it grazes in the Rutulian forests and on the domain of Turnus; Caesar's herd is not ready to obey ordinary citizens, though their ancestors used to obey Tyrian Hannibal and our own generals and King Molossus and carried cohorts aback, a large unit, and a turret when going into battle.]

Holyday's versification here is even more slapdash than usual, as if he thought the passage required simplicity verging on idiocy.

> . . . Some a *Hecatombe* will vow;
> Since th' Elephant's no *Latian* ware. Indeed
> That Beast under our Stars does no where feed:
> But brought from swarthy Nations they are rear'd
> In the *Rutilian* Forest. *Caesars* Heard
> Sleights Subjects: *Tyrian Hannibal* they obey'd;
> Our Gen'rals and great *Pyrrhus* they did aid.
> Their Sires did on their backs carry a Pow'r
> Of Souldiers, and a Warlike Marching Tow'r.   [p. 230]

Holyday shows no sign of having caught Juvenal's satirical point, a failure that we can hardly censure, because most later critics of Juvenal have been equally at a loss and assumed that in his later years his always-shaky command of structure abandoned him completely. Actually the passage sorts quite well with a principal theme of most of the satires, modern degeneracy vis-à-vis antique virtue. In Juvenal's time elephants no longer served in war; former symbols of the military might of Rome's enemies (that is, Hannibal and Pyrrhus) were now useless pets in the emperor's private zoo.[8]

Although he missed the point on elephants, Holyday was alert to the moral applications of Juvenal's satires. He ended his translation of the satires with "Trin-Uni Deo Gloria" (Glory be to the Three-Personed God) and the Illustrations with "Laus Deo" (Praise be to God"). Although traditionally Horace was regarded as the exemplar of private morality, whereas Juvenal dealt with the high crimes and misdemeanors of public personalities, several of Juvenal's satires had something to offer ordinary readers in search of advice. The tenth and the thirteenth satires were the most esteemed; after them the most relevant to personal ethics were the eighth, on social snobbery, and the fourteenth, on the proper education of children. With seemingly modern insight, Juvenal argues that children acquire their vices by imitating their parents, particularly those who teach their children to be misers. As Juvenal draws toward the end he invokes perhaps the most enduring of the satiric topoi, that all the wealth one needs is what satisfies Nature's minimum requirements for shelter, warmth, and food.

Tantis parta malis cura maiore metuque
servantur; misera est magni custodia census.
dispositis praedives amis vigilare cohortem
servorum noctu Licinus iubet, attonitus pro
electro signisque suis Phrygiaque columna
atque ebore et lata testudine. dolia nudi
non ardent Cynici; si fregeris, altera fiet
cras domus atque eadem plumbo commissa manebit.
sensit Alexander, testa cum vidit in illa
magnum habitatorem, quanto felicior hic qui
nil cuperet quam qui totum sibi posceret orbem
passurus gestis aequanda pericula rebus.
nullum numen habes, si sit prudentia: nos te,
nos facimus, Fortuna, deam. mensura tamen quae
sufficiat census, si quis me consulat, edam:
in quantum sitis atque fames et frigora poscunt,
quantum, Epicure, tibi parvis suffecit in hortis,
quantum Socratici ceperunt ante penates.   [303-20]

[Things gained at great cost are kept with greater care and fear; preserving a huge fortune is miserable. Rich Licinus orders a cohort of slaves to watch at night with fire-buckets at the ready, fearing for his amber and his statues and his Phrygian columns and his ivory and his broad tortoise shells. The jars of the naked Cynic don't burn; if you break one, another house is ready tomorrow, or the same one patched with lead. Alexander felt, when he saw the great inhabitant of that jar, how much happier the one who desired nothing was than the one who wanted the whole world for himself, taking on dangers as great as his deeds. If we had prudence, you would have no divinity: we, O Fortune, we make you a goddess. If someone asks me what would be enough, I'll tell him: As much as thirst, hunger, and cold demand; as much as sufficed for you, O Epicurus, in your little garden; as much as Socrates' household consumed.]

Where Juvenal's style is restrained, as here, Holyday shows himself at his best.

Wealth got with much care must be kept with more:
To Guard great Treasure's worse than to be poor.
By night the Rich *Licinus* made a Guard
Of Servants with their buckets watch and ward:
His Amber, Statues, Phrygian Columns, rare
Ivory and large shells, wrought with such frightning care.
The naked Cynicks tub ne're burn'd: if broken
'Twas leaded, or a New was straight bespoken.
When *Alexander* in that Cell did see
That Great Inhabitant, more pleas'd was he,
He thought, that nothing wish'd, then he that fain
With worlds of dangers would the whole world gain.
The Gods are all ours, if we're wise: but we
Make thee a Goddess, *Fortune*! yet if me
One asks, what size of wealth is fit, I'le tell:
As much as will Thirst, Hunger, Cold expell;
What serv'd Thee, *Epicurus*, Hearbs small store;
What *Socrates* his House-Gods ask'd before.   [pp. 258-59]

Some of the syntax is tortured, particularly "yet if me / One asks" and "*Socrates* his House-Gods ask'd before." "Phrygian Columns, rare / Ivory, and large shells" might not sound so anti-climactic to a reader who did not think immediately of the beach, and Juvenal would have loved Holyday's having Diogenes' "tub" "straight bespoken."[9] But Holyday also uses some rhetorical flourishes to elevate his style: Licinus' servants form a "watch and ward" and Alexander "With worlds of dangers would the whole world gain." "What . . . What" corresponds to Juvenal's anaphora "quantum . . . quantum."

Although by the standards of the 1690s Holyday's translation was hopelessly old-fashioned, it is quite respectable for its time.

What sounds like grossly excessive enjambment to an ear trained on the Augustans probably seemed elegant then—as we shall see, Henry Vaughan uses it even more. And Holyday's syntax is no more distorted than Milton's. Many modern verse translators have done worse.

[II]

Seventeenth-century editions containing both Juvenal and Persius invariably placed Persius at the end—even though he precedes Juvenal chronologically—as if he were some sort of satiric afterthought. The same is true in the 1673 edition of Holyday's translation. Persius' style gave Holyday a chance to try his hand at the conversational couplet (and if he seems clumsy by the standard set by Alexander Pope, try comparing Holyday's Persius to the verse epistles of John Donne before judging). Persius employed the *sermo pedestris* of Horace, but, unlike Horace's bankrupt art collectors and newly converted slaves, the Stoic philosophers in Persius are the real thing, high-minded types ready to criticize our disgusting habits in detail. In the third satire a tutor finds his pupil still sleeping off a debauch at eleven in the morning.

" . . . iam clarum mane fenestras
intrat et angustas extendit lumine rimas:
stertimus indomitum quod despumare Falernum
sufficiat, quinta dum linea tangitur umbra.
en quid agis? siccas insana canicula messes
iam dudum coquit et patula pecus omne sub ulmo est."

["The clear light is already coming through the windows and widening the cracks between the blinds. We're snoring away to sleep off the strong Falernian wine when the shadow (of the sundial) touches the fifth line. And what are you doing? The raging Dog Star has already baked the wheat dry and the entire herd is under the spreading elm."]

Holyday is more leisurely. Unlike in his method for Juvenal, he makes no attempt to render the original line for line.

... fie, fie, arise:
See how the clear light shamefully descries
Thy sloth: and through thy windows shining bright
Stretcheth the narrow chinks with his broad light.
We snort till the Fift shadow touch the line,
Enough ev'n to digest strong *Falerne* wine.
Now what dost do? The furious dog-stars heat
Upon the parched corn hath long since beat
With its fierce scalding influence, and made
The Beasts to seek the spreading *Elmes* cool shade.   [p. 309]

The "fie, fie," and "Now what dost do?" have the right colloquial tone. "We snort" for "stertimus" is literally accurate, but lacks the force of what might be called the "noninclusive we" (Gildersleeve calls it the "Ironical First Person, excluding the speaker"),[10] with its implication of insufferable superiority so typical of nannies, teachers, and pet owners. One could object to "beat / With its fiece scalding influence" as too literary and paraphrastic for "coquit," but "to seek the spreading *Elmes* cool shade" is fine for "patula ... sub ulmo," with its echo of the opening line of Virgil's *Eclogues*. Literary echoes are a bane to translators, but worse are popularized technicalities, especially technicalities from discredited pseudosciences.[11] One of the cardinal tenets of Stoicism is that fate is forever fixed, so a deterministic system such as astrology had considerable appeal. Or as A. E. Housman put it in his inimitable manner: "There was little star-gazing in Epicurus' sty; but the Stoics, enamoured of divinity and not much attached to truth, had been carried away captive by the daughter of Babylon; and many of the hours which Persius and [his tutor] Cornutus devoted to common study were spent in acquiring Mesopotamian misinformation about celestial objects."[12] The fifth satire, a dialogue between Persius and Cornutus, attempts to prove that favorite Stoic paradox that however exalted your political or social status, if you are not a sage you are really merely a slave. Because teachers, especially those attached to doctrinaire systems, love to see themselves reincarnated in their students, Cornutus must have beamed when Persius assured him that their minds were so alike that the same astrological conjunction must be responsible.

tecum etenim longos memini consumere soles,
et tecum primas epulis decerpere noctes:
unum opus et requiem pariter disponimus ambo,
atque verecunda laxamus seria mensa.
non equidem hoc dubites, amborum foedere certo
consentire dies et ab uno sidere duci.
nostra vel aequali suspendit tempora Libra
Parca tenax veri, seu nata fidelibus hora
dividit in Geminos concordia fata duorum,
Saturnumque gravem nostro Iove frangimus una:
nescio quod certe est quod me tibi temperat astrum.   [41-51]

[Indeed, I recall spending the long days with you, and with you snatched the early hours of evening for feasting: we both gave ourselves to the same work and to the same rest, and relaxed from cares at the same modest table. You should not doubt that both our nativities are joined by fixed accord and are ruled by the same star. Whether Fate suspended our time of birth in the equal scales (that is, under Libra) or whether she divided the natal hour for faithful friends between the Gemini, we offset malign Saturn with Jupiter. Certainly some star, whatever it was, made me just like you.]

It was probably to Holyday's advantage that many "people of 'culture' " in the seventeenth century still believed in astrology,[13] though I wonder how many would recall offhand that the *Parcae* are the three fates.

For I remember oft I with delight
Have spent long days with Thee: and of the Night
Have borrow'd the first hours, feasting with thee
On the choise dainties of Philosophie.
One work we wrought: we rested both one rest:
Mixing severeness with a modest jest.
For doubt not, both our birth-days joyn'd in one
Sure league, drawn from one constellation:
Or the unchanged *Parca* weigh'd our time

> With an ev'n ballance: or that first, that prime
> Birth-hour of us true friends did blessedly
> Place our embracing fates in *Gemini:*
> And heavy *Saturnes* stern malignity
> Was broke by our good *Joves* benignity.
> I know not what, but sure some Star I see,
> Which inwardly disposes me towards Thee.   [pp. 324-25]

Holyday could safely expect his reader to understand that Persius has metaphorical rather than astrological reasons for suggesting Libra and Gemini as appropriate signs. Both represent harmony and agreement. Saturn must have influenced Persius' and Cornutus' love of study, but Jupiter would have made them cheerful and agreeable, not Saturnine melancholic grumps.

   Persius was a ideal poet for the young Holyday to attempt to translate. As a valetudinarian and a recluse who drew most of his inspiration from books, Persius' reputation for obscurity must have exerted the same fascination on a young scholar eager to prove his virtuosity to antiquaries, learned poets, and scholars that Ezra Pound and T. S. Eliot exerted on a later generation. And his reputation for hobbling verse made the quaintness of Holyday's couplets scarcely a drawback. In fact, Holyday gave the English reader a fair idea of what it is like to read Persius in Latin.

George Chapman's and John Biddle's Translations from Juvenal

The year 1629 was important in the history of satire in England, as it marks the first time a professional translator turned his hand to a Roman satirist. George Chapman's stature as a poet is ambiguous. His tragedies are full of elevated neo-Stoical pieties uttered by characters about to commit treachery, his poems *The Shadow of Night*, *Andromeda Liberata*, and *Ovid's Banquet of Sense* are obscure, and his comedies are scarcely read today except by graduate students looking for a dissertation topic. He is best-known for his versions of Homer (*Iliad*, 1612, *Odyssey*, 1615), in which Keats thought he heard "Chapman speak out loud and bold." His translation of the fifth satire of Juvenal, which seems to have aroused little scholarly interest,[1] was buried in an obscure publication with the odd title *A Justification of a Strange Action of Nero; in Burying with a Solemne Funerall, One of the Cast Hayres of His Mistresse Poppaea. Also a Iust Reproofe of a Romane Smell-feast, Being the Fifth Satyre of Juvenall*. The former is a prose piece purporting to be a speech by the Emperor Nero himself, and perhaps it was the seventeeth-century habit of bracketing Juvenal's denunciation of Imperial depravity with the reign of Nero, as well as that of Domitian, that made Chapman think that a version of one of Juvenal's satires would make an appropriate companion piece.

The fifth satire is at once Juvenal's most biting and most delightful. It is devoted to a subject satirists through the ages find inexhaustable, the horrible party. In classical satire the the host is often a nouveau riche vulgarian, such as Nasidienus in Horace's eighth satire of the second book or Trimalchio in Petronius' *Satyricon*. Juvenal gives the traditional subject a new twist. His host is unpleasant enough, a rich man named Virro, perhaps the same Virro as the wealthy pathic of the ninth satire, but the main target is not the ostentation and vulgarity of the host, but the fawning behavior of the prospective guest, a client named Trebius, whom his master means to humiliate. Juvenal offers his usual extreme alternatives. This time he suggests that Trebius could do better to feed himself by begging or on a diet of kennel ration ("sordes farris mordere canini," 11), then warns him that if he accepts Virro's invitation it is last favor he can ever expect.

Primo fige loco, quod tu discumbere iussus
mercedem solidam veterum capis officiorum.
fructus amicitiae magnae cibus, inputat hunc rex,
et quamvis rarum tamen inputat. . . .   [12-15]

[First remember this, that when you are ordered to recline (at table) you take the whole reward for all your former services. The food is the fruit of the great friendship; the patron will deem it so and however rarely you are invited continue to so regard it.]

Turning to Chapman's translation of the fifth satire, we can see clearly that there has been something of a breakthrough.

First, take it for a Rule, that if my Lord
Shall once be pleas'd to grace thee with his bord,
The whole reuenewes that thy hopes inherit
Rising from seruices of ancient merit,
In this requitall amply paid will prooue.
O 'tis the fruit of a transcendent loue,
To giue one victuals; That, thy Table-King
Layes in thy dish, though nere so thinne a thing,
Yet that reproach, still in thine eares shall ring.   [pp. 12-13]

Despite the unidiomatic "Table-King"—a too-literal attempt at the Latin "rex"—the diction is much closer to colloquial English than anything earlier translators could manage. Chapman also knows how to use versification to reinforce meaning. The anticlimactic descent to "victuals,"[2] with its semicolon stop at the hemistich and enjambment leading into a triplet whose extra line brings out the repeated nagging of the host, is worthy of Dryden. Chapman's "reuenewes" (apparently accented on the second syllable), and "requitall" nicely catch Juvenal's metaphor that Virro regards one bad meal as the final reward for Trebius' lifetime of servility.

Just how bad a meal it is we discover in one of the most brilliant narratives in satiric literature. In a detailed description of each course, Juvenal begins with the wine list. Trebius is served a cheap plonk that even oily wool—which the Romans used for rubdowns—would refuse to absorb ("vinum quod sucida nolit / lana pati"). Virro

ipse capillato diffusum consule potat
calcatamque tenet bellis socialibus uvam,
cardiaco numquam cyanthus missurus amico.
cras bibet Albanis aliquid de montibus aut de
Setinis, cuius patriam titulumque senectus
delevit multa veteris fuligine testae,
quale coronati Thrasea Helvidiusque bibebant
Brutorum et Cassi natalibus. . . .   [30-37]

[He drinks wine bottled when the consuls wore long hair, the grapes were crushed during the Social Wars; he would never offer the cup to a friend with heartburn. Tomorrow he will drink something from the Alban hills or from Setia from a bottle so old that the label is unreadable under the mold, such as Thrasea and Helvidius drank celebrating the birthdays of the Brutuses and Cassius.]

Pedantry was one of Chapman's less endearing traits, and he seems to be trying to use more "classical" allusions than Juvenal himself.

For *Virro's*-selfe, the wine he drinks was borne
When Consuls (*Phoebus*-like) appear'd vnshorn,
A Grape that long since in the wars was prest

By our confederate-*Marsians*, and the rest
Of which, no drop his longing-frend can git
Though blowne in fume vp with a Cardiack fit.
Next day he likes to taste another field,
The *Albane* hills, or els the *Setine* yeeld
Whose race and rich succession if you aske,
Age hath decayd, and sicknesse of the caske,
Such *Thrasea* & *Heluidius* quaft, stil crownd
When *Brutus* birth, and *Cassius* they renownd.   [p. 14]

Dragging in Apollo by his long hair does nothing to convey
Juvenal's point to the English reader, that a hispid countenance
was associated with the early days of the Roman Republic. Nor
does that reader need to know that the Social Wars were so called
because they were fought against the Roman's "socii," the Marsians; we do need to know that those wars were fought in the early
years of the first century B.C. Virro's wine would be more than
two hundred years old! Hyperbole, of course. The point is that
these are "vins d'une qualité exceptionnelle."³ Chapman's contemporaries would not, however, be misled by "Cardiack fit"; like the
original's "cardiaco" it does not mean a "heart attack" but rather
"heartburn."⁴ Thrasea and Helvidius need to be identified too.
They were Stoic aristocrats condemned for plotting to assassinate
Nero. Presumably only the best would do on birthdays of their
heroes, the liberators who killed Julius Caesar.

Despite the obscurity of the allusions, the style of Chapman's
verse is impressive, carrying with it no sense of strain, no sense
that Chapman is having any trouble accommodating his alien
original to English couplets. Yet, he catches the flow of the Latin
well. Two three-couplet units each correspond to a period in the
original, and Chapman supplies strong stops only at the end of the
period. (Given the vagaries of early seventeenth-century printers—and this printer was more careless than most—I would not
venture to say which lines are enjambed. I should think "rest / Of
which" is an enjambment, but am tempted to put a comma after
"yeeld" for a short pause.)

Chapman was the first translator of a Roman satirist to show he clearly understood that different languages must use different methods to achieve similar effects. As he says in his dedication, perhaps with Ben Jonson in mind:

Because in most opinions of translation, a most asinine error hath gotten eare and head, that men must attempt it as a mastery in rendring any originall into other language, to doe it in as few words, and the like order; I thought it not amisse in this pore portion of translation; to pick out (like the rotten out of Apples if you please to repute it) a poore instance or two that endeauour to demonstrate a right in the contrary. And the rather I take this course ocularily to present you with example of what I esteeme fit to saue the liberty and dialect of mine owne language; because there are many valetudinaries, that neuer know the goodnesse of their sto-macke till they see meat afore them.[5]

Chapman has some nice touches that work only in English. The lobster served Virro is so huge that it is too big for its platter ("aspice quam longo distendat pectore lancem" [behold how he extends the platter with his long chest, 80]—modern texts of Juvenal usually read "distinguat" for "distendat") and so Chapman invites us to note: "How with the length of his extended limbes / He does surcharge the Charger ... " (p. 17). Trebius is served a pale wretched little cabbage smelling of lamp oil ("pallidus affertur misero tibi caulis, olebit / lanternam," 87-88). Chapman expands this passage to read:

But, for the Worts (poore snake) presented thee,
Whose pale aspect, shewes their infirmity;
They drinke an oyle, much of the Curriers stamp,
Exquisite stuffe, that sauours of the lamp.   [p. 18]

I think Juvenal would have been amused at the idea of Trebius' salad dressing tasting like neat's-foot oil.

Roman gluttons were mad about huge fish (Juvenal's fourth satire is devoted to the subject), and Virro dines on an enormous mullet followed by a gigantic lamprey.

Virroni muraena datur, quae maxima venit
gurgite de Siculo; nam dum se continet Auster,

dum sedet et siccat madidas in carcere pinnas,
contemnunt mediam temeraria lina Charybdim.
vos anguilla manet longae cognata colubrae,
aut glacie aspersus maculis Tiberinus, et ipse
vernula riparum, pinguis torrente cloaca
et solitus mediae cryptam penetrare Suburae.   [99-107]

[A moray is given to Virro, a huge one which came from the Sicilian whirlpool, for while Auster (the southwind) restrains himself, while he sits and dries his wings in prision, the daring nets make light to the middle of Charybdis. An eel awaits you, the kin of a long snake, or a fish bred in the Tiber, speckled with ice, a denizen of the riverbanks fat from the roaring sewer and a regular visitor to the drain in the middle of Subura (the slum district of Rome).]

We begin with allusions to epic—the Aeolian prison of the winds and Charybdis—and end up in the satirist's world of the slums and the sewers. As one would expect of the translator of Homer, Chapman has no trouble with the heroic touches.

In messe with that [the mullet], behold for *Virro* lies
A *Lamprey* of an exemplary Size,
That for dimension beares the price from all
Which Gulphes *Sicilian* sent his Festiuall,
For while the South conteynes himselfe; while he
Lies close, and dries his feathers in his Lee,
Our greedy Pursenets for their gaine despise
The danger that in mid *Charibdis* lies.
    Now, for his *Lamprey*, thou art glad to take
An *Eele*, neere cozen to a hideous Snake,
Or els a freckled-*Tiberine*, bit with frost,
And he, the poorest slaue of all the coast;
Fed with the torrent of the common Sewer,
And swims the towne-ditch, (where 'tis most impure).   [p. 19]

The rolling quadrisyllable "exemplary" seems to enlarge Virro's moray, also dignified by the epic inversion "Gulphes *Sicilian*." "South" for the south wind was a standard piece of poetic diction in the seventeenth and eighteenth centuries and the conceit that has the south wind drying his feathers in his own lee is a delicious Ovidian touch. Appropriately, Trebius' eel is described in much more prosaic language as "neere cozen to a hideous Snake." Translating "vernula" (literally, a slave born to one's household, thus generally of lower quality than the fancy imported item) as "poorest slaue" seems too literal to be idiomatic and effective, but "common Sewer" and "towne-ditch" rightly replacing Juvenal's more precise topography are the kinds of paraphrases the English reader needs.

Unfortunately, Chapman seems never to have carried out his plan and translated any more of Juvenal's satires. Chapman brought to Juvenal an ear for smooth-sounding verse, a feeling for elevated diction, and the contrasting keen sense of the ridiculous and taste for the ironic. No later translator seems to have laid eyes on Chapman's version of the fifth satire, not surprisingly, since it was buried in such an odd and fugitive publication. Were it better known, the seventeenth-century misapprehension that "satyr" demands a rough and crude style might have been overturned sooner than it was.

[II]

Unlike Horatians, who seem to pass cheerfully through life never more than five minutes late for a hot dinner, Juvenal's admirers often have very unhappy lives, and I wonder if in 1634 when the young John Biddle, still a schoolboy (he was born in 1615), published *Virgil's Bucolicks Englished Whereunto is Added the Translation of the Two First Satyrs of Juvenal* he ever suspected that his devotion to scholarship would ultimately lead to imprisonment—in the Isles of Scilly—for daring to publish a book questioning the godhead of the Holy Ghost. Biddle may have planned to translate the rest of Juvenal. In an "Epistle" to readers prefaced to the translation of the first two satires, he wrote:

Marvell not, Readers, that I set before you but this Pittance: I was loth to cloy your Appetites at the first, knowing (on the one side) that mens quesy and squemish stomacks rellish better the poinant suckets of a

Love-Sonnet, or the Iulips [yes, as in mint juleps] of a frothy Epigram, than a Homely (though holesom [*sic*]) dish of Satyricall stuffe: And fearing withall (on t'other side) lest having cooked a great deale of this hard and sower-Meat ill, I might have so distasted a truely judicious Palat, as to have made it even sicke with Loathing, being not able by Reason of the Quality (much more the Quantity) without great annoyance, to concoct it. In this therefore (in cooking I meane) if I have greatly failed, I will willing cry *Peccavi*, and herein offend no more: if not, (God helping) present you with the second and third course. In the mean-time, Gentlemen, rest you content. (C4v)

The comparison of a translated satire to a dish sounds like Chapman's, but the metaphor is implicit in the etymology of *satura*, so there is no reason to believe Biddle could not have thought of it himself; I can think of no one else who presses the comparison of composing poetry to cooking quite so far. The tone of the "Epistle" sounds a bit cheeky, what one might expect of a bright eighteen-year-old showing off, and the the translation bears out that impression. In the first satire Juvenal's "Frontonis platani convulsaque marmora clamant / semper et adsiduo ruptae lectore columnae" (the plane trees and marble of Fronto continually cry out as well as the columns broken by constant recitation, 12-13) inspired Biddle's

Muse-fostring *Fronto's* walks his Or-thards round,
Seeld with broad-spreading Plane-Trees, still resound.
And's Roof's ev'n shivered downe with oft Repeating,
And Marble Columnes with the daily Beating
Of yelling Poets cryes ev'n broke, record,
As if th'had conn'd it over every Word.   [C5v]

It appears that Biddle decided that he had no chance of imitating Juvenal's compression, and tried instead to make Juvenal even more hyperbolical by exaggerating the destructive capacity of bad poetry. Our initial impression that Biddle is in no hurry is borne out in the rest of his version, which is 334 lines long—a possible record for translations of the first satire. (Dryden's runs to 258 lines.) But unlike the egregious Barksted, Biddle is under control and when he translates a line does not have to search desperately to make up another one to rhyme with it. Rather, he seems to enjoy inventing new details and examples, packing them as tight as he can, as his elisions show.

Biddle is just as playful when he comes to Juvenal's description of the wealthy miser who sends all his poor clients home so that he keep all the gourmet treats for himself.

vestibulis abeunt veteres lassique clientes
votaque deponunt, quamquam longissima cenae
spes homini: caules miseris atque ignis emendus.
optima silvarum interea pelagi vorabit
rex horum vacuisque toris tantum ipse iacebit.
nam de tot pulcris and latis orbibus et tam
antiquis una comedunt patrimonia mensa.
nullus iam parasitus erit. sed quis ferat istas
luxuriae sordes? quanta est gula quae sibi totos
ponit apros, animal propter convivia natum!
poena tamen praesens, cum tu deponis amictus
turgidus et crudum pavonem in balnea portas.
hinc subitae mortes atque intesta senectus.
it nova nec tristis per cunctas fabula cenas:
ducitur iratis plaudendum funus amicis.   [132-46]

[The tired old clients depart and put aside their prayers, although the longest human hope is for a dinner: a fire and miserable cabbages must be purchased. Meanwhile the king himself will devour the choicest fruits of the woods and seas and will recline alone with empty cushions. For from so many beautiful and wide and old tables they devour patrimonies in one meal. No freeloader will be present. But who could endure this niggardly luxury? So great is his gullet that he serves himself entire boars, an animal intended for a banquet. Punishment follows straightway, when stuffed you put aside your cloak and carry in your belly the undigested peacock into the bath. Hence quick death and intestate old age. A new and amusing story goes through all the dinner tables and your funeral will be cheered by your irate friends.]

Again, Biddle movers slower and supplies new details borrowed from the commentary in Thomas Farnaby's popular schooltext.[6]

... The Old weary Clients then, dismist,
Depart the Lobby, with a Maund content,
(That for a Supper hop't before they went)
And with it (for they quite despaire againe)
To buy 'em Wood, and Cole worts last are faine.
　　Meanewhile the choicest Sea fish, at his Boord,
The choicest Ven'son that the Woods afford,
Their Kingly Patron rich doth gurmandize,
And by Himselfe on his Bed empty lyes:
For of so many Faire, so Old, and Large,
They but when Table still with Viands charge,
Their Patrimonies ther devouring quite.
There will be now no Smell-feast Parasite.
But who'l endure those base Luxurious Chuffes?
Whole Brawns before him sets (Prodigious thing!)
A Creature onely made for Banqueting?
But Thou dost quickly for thy Ravening pay:
For when Thou, stripped, downe thy Robes dost lay,
And to the Bath within thy strouting Panch
(The which so many Cates before did stanch)
An undigested Peacocks Flesh dost bring,
Hence sudden Deaths, and Age Intestate spring.
A Now (nor Balefull) Fame is bruited, Beast;
Of thy untimely Death at every Feast.
And thy last Funerall Solemnitie
Is by thy moody Friends performed with Glee.　　　[D1r–D1v]

It is easier to spot levels of style in Latin, where there is generally a clear line between literary and vulgar usage, than in earlier English, where words now obsolete or dialectic, such as "Cates," "Brawns," and "moody" (in the sense of "angry") sound quaint and homely to us, though they may not have to Biddle's original audience. Whatever Biddle's original audience thought of the style, I doubt that they would have perceived much of Juvenal's famous *indignatio* coming through. Juvenal relies on speed and surprise; Biddle on laboriously setting up each couplet (the epithet "Beast" to rhyme with "Feast" is particularly crude). Perhaps Biddle's experience with patronage—at age ten he had been allowed ten pounds a year by Lord Berkeley—was happier than Juvenal's or Samuel Johnson's.

The first satire is a natural choice for a young poetic translator trying to show what he can do, but it must have required some nerve to take on Juvenal's second satire. It starts off with an attack on a sect of Stoic hypocrites who pretend to the utmost austerity in morals and demeanor while secretly indulging in homosexual orgies. Warns Juvenal:

frontis nulla fides; quis enim non vicus abundat
tristibus obscaenis? castigas turpia, cum sis
inter Socraticos notissima fossa cinaedos?
hispida membra quidem et durae per braccia saetae
promittunt atrocem animum, sed podice levi
caeduntur tumidae medico ridente mariscae.
rarus sermo illis et magna libido tacendi
atque supercilio brevior coma. verius ergo
et magis ingenue Peribomius: hunc ego fatis
inputo, qui voltu morbum incessuque fatetur.
horum simplicitas miserabilis, his furor ipse
dat veniam: sed peiiores, qui talia verbis
Herculis invadunt et de virtute locuti
clunem agitant. "ego te ceventem, Sexte, verebor?"
infamis Varillus ait "quo deterior te?
loripedem rectus derideat, Aethiopem albus!"   [7-23]

[Don't trust in appearance: what neighborhood does not abound in stern-looking perverts? Do you censure shameful deeds, while you're the best-known crevice among the Socratic queers? Hairy legs, indeed, and rough bristles on the arms proclaim an ascetic disposition, but swelling piles are sliced from your smooth buttocks by the laughing doctor. Among them there is little speech and a great love of being silent and hair shorter than their eyebrows. Peribomius is freer and more honest about it: I attribute him to fate, he who by his face and his walk proclaims the disease. Their wretched condition is open, madness gives them an excuse. But much worse are those who attack such practices with Herculean words and talk about virtue while they shake their butt. "Am I to be in awe of you, Sextus, while you wiggle your arse?" says the infamous Varillus, "how am I worse than you? Let the hale make fun of the cripple, the white of the Ethiopian?"]

As in the first satire, Biddle's version develops more slowly.

The Front's a cozening Mirror: For what street
Is not with Obscene *Catoes* now repleate?
None more comptrols Effeminacy, than
The most notorious soft *Socratian.*
Rough Limbs, and Armes all-bristled o'r with Haire,
Are the plaine Badges of a Mind severe:
But in thy smooth Posteriors, full of Biles,
The smiling Leach doth lance the swelling Piles.
   These men have seal'd-up Lips, and take great Pride,
In silence and demurnesse; yea, beside
Their notted Haire doth not their Ey-brow busse:
And therefore debaucht *Peribonius*[7]
Is in a far more tolerable state;
His Nature to Malignant Stars, and Fate
I iustly doe impute, whose very colour,
And lazy Gate are Symptomes of his Dolour.
Such mens simplicity should Vs excite
To Sympathy, and Ruth; Their Passion's might
Doth plead them Guiltlesse: But far worse are They
Who with *Herculean* Thundring Taunts inveigh
'Gainst these Delinquents, and of Vertue prate
Amid their base Venereous Cringes. What?
For feare of thy drad presence shall I shiver,
While thy Posteriors do obscenely quiver:
Or, *Sextus,* am I one jot worse than Thee,
Quoth loose *Varillus* of known Infamy?
Strait let Him be, that mocks a wry-leg'd Man;
White, that derides an *Æthiopian.*   [D2r]

"Base Venereous Cringes" resembles the kind of "translationese" bowdlerizers fall back on, but "Posteriors do obscenely quiver" catches fairly well Juvenal's "ceventem" (which Farnaby glossed as "clunes agitatem"). Biddle uses doublets to slow his verse and fill out his couplets. Most, such as "Sympathy, and Ruth," "known Infamy," and "silence and demurenesse" are pleonastic, but "Malignant Stars, and Fate" brings out a meaning implicit in Juvenal's "fatis"—the ancients assumed one's sexual orientation was determined astrologically.

Like most other early couplet translators, Biddle seems unaware of the possiblities of closure, of using the rhymes for emphasis. But he uses feminine endings—such as "shiver/quiver"—more often than other translators, and not, I think, because he was either careless or incompetent. Feminine rhymes sound jaunty and irreverent in iambic pentameter, perhaps because the extra unstressed syllable makes us feel that the poet is not taking his work seriously. They are not especially common in Biddle, but he uses them often enough to lighten the tone, as in his version of verses 149-52, where Juvenal remarks that nobody believes in hell anymore.

Esse aliquos manes and subterranea regna
et contum et Stygio ranas in gurgite nigras
atque una transire vadum tot milia cumba
nec pueri credunt, nisi qui nondum aere lavantur.

[That there are such things as ghosts and underground realms and a punt-pole and black frogs in the Stygian whirlpool and that so many thousands are ferried across in one boat not even boys believe, unless they are too young to have to pay a penny to get into the baths.]

That there are any grizly, hideous Ghoasts;
Realms vnder ground in Hel's black Ebon Coasts;
And a long shoving Pole (grim *Charon's* Oare;)
And blacke Frogs swimming in the *Stygian* Moore,
And that so many thousand souls do float,
And stem that Sable Sound in one small Boat;
Men, nay even Boyes themselves (vnlesse they be)
No higher than three Horse-loaves, nor a Fee
E'r to the Bath-guide did for Batting pay)
Are so farre from Beleeving Now, that They
But Silly Old wives Fables do esteem 'em,
And childrens Bugs, and Scare-crows onely deem 'em.   [D7r]

Again, some of Biddle's additions are straight from Farnaby—"grim *Charon's* Oare" from the note on "contum," "Quo Charon ratem subigit" and "Silly Old wives Fables do esteem 'em" closely follows "fabulas esse aniles credant omnes." Like Juvenal, Biddle mixes elevated poetic diction—"Ebon Coasts," "*Stygian* Moore, and "Sable Sound"—with such low commonplace expressions as "Bugs" and "Scare-crows." "No higher than three Horse-loaves" may be proverbial.[8] Despite the attempt in the seventeenth century to divide the genus of satire into the comic and tragic species, and to assign the former to Horace and the latter to Juvenal, Juvenal has a keen sense of the ridiculous that many seventeenth-century translators missed. Biddle seems to be the first (though there are funny moments in Chapman) translator to make us feel that he had fun reading Juvenal and turning him into English.

Juvenal and Horace in the Civil War and Interregnum

Scholars have not written much about Sir Robert Stapleton's translation of Juvenal, perhaps rightly, as Stapleton was not much better a poet than Holyday, whom he beat to the press by nearly thirty years. But Stapleton was not only the first to publish translations of all of the satires into English, he was also the first translator of a Roman satirist to publish revisions, although few have noticed them. No less than five editions of his Juvenal were published, and three of them offer substantively different texts.

The first was published in 1644 at Oxford, then the headquarters of the Royalist forces. Stapleton held the post of Gentleman in Ordinary of the Privy Chamber of the Prince, the future Charles II, a task that must have left him with a good deal of time on his hands.[1] His uncle, the Earl of Kingston, was a counselor to King Charles I, and was apparently the one who suggested that Stapleton take on Juvenal. Stapleton also had access to the papers of Barten Holyday.[2] The first edition was entitled *The First Six Satyrs of Juvenal with Annotations Clearing the Obscurer Places out of the History, Lawes, and Ceremonies of the Romans*, "Printed by Hen. Hall for *Thomas Robinson*." Two years later a similar octavo was published in London, now called *The Satyrs of Juvenal* and informing readers that it was "Printed for *Humphrey Moseley*, and are to be sold at his shop at the Signe of the Princes Armes in St. *Pauls* Churchyard." This "edition" is in fact the Oxford edition of 1644 with leaves A1 and A2 canceled. Moseley's purpose is not clear, but I suspect he was ensuring that he secured copyright against the day that Stapleton finished translating the rest of the satires. That must have been soon, for in 1647 Moseley published Stapleton's *Juvenal's Sixteen Satyrs, or, a Survey of the Manners and Actions of Mankind,* similar in format to 1646, but of course thicker. It is this edition that is most often found today. Yet no one has remarked that Stapleton revised his 1644 translation of the first six satires slightly for the 1647 version. More important, he was to publish an extensively reworked version in 1660. Although Stapleton's second and third thoughts did not carry him much further up the foothills of Parnassus, they do give us some evidence of what was happening in translation during a crucial period of transition in the development of English poetry.

In the famous opening of the third satire, Juvenal tells how he feels about the departure from Rome of his friend Umbricius, who is looking for some place more hospitable to an honest man:

Quamvis digressu veteris confusus amici,
laudo tamen, vacuis quod sedem figere Cumis
destinet atque unum civem donare Sibyllae.
ianua Baiarum est et gratum litus amoeni
secessus. ego vel Prochytam praepono Suburae;
nam quid tam miserum, tam solum vidimus, ut non
deterius credas horrere incendia, lapsus
tectorum adsiduos ad mille pericula saevae
urbis et Augusto recitantes mense poetas?
sed dum tota domus raeda componitur una,
substitit ad veteres arcus madidamque Capenam.
hic ubi nocturae Numa constituebat amicae—
nunc sacri fontis nemus et delubra locantur
Iudaeis quorum cophinus faenum supellex,
omnis enim populo mercedem pendere iussa est
arbor et eiectis mendicat silva Camenis.

[However upset by the departure of an old friend, I praise him nevertheless, because he plans to settle in empty Cumae and give a citizen to the Sybil. It is the gateway to Baiae and the pleasant shore of a pretty bay. I should prefer even Prochyta (a barren island) to the Subura; for what place do we see that is so wretched, so lonely, that you wouldn't think it worse to be terrified by fires, the constant fall of buildings, but also the thousand dangers of the savage city and poets reciting in the month of August? But when his household had been packed into one wagon, he stood under the ancient arches and damp Capena. Here where Numa used to meet his nocturnal girlfriend—now the grove of the sacred fountain and the temple are leased to Jewish beggars who own only a basket and some straw, for every tree is required to pay rent to the public and the woods are beggars now that the Muses are banished.]

Although the translation of Juvenal was not Stapleton's maiden effort (he had already published a translation of the fourth book of the *Aeneid* in 1634), he had far to go to become a competent poet. But though his opening of the third satire is hardly elegant, it is efficient.

> Though my old friend's Remove my soule doth wound,
> I joy that he's for empty *Cuma* bound
> On *Sybil* to bestow one Dweller more.
> 'Tis th'entrance to the Bath, a pleasant shore
> For sweete retirement: ev'n their *Prochytas*
> Does our *Suburra* in my minde surpasse.
> For what's so lonely, wretched, horrid there;
> As frights of fire, still falling houses here?
> And thousand dangers this curste Towne must dread,
> Besides the Poets that in *August* read.
> The waggon, wherein all his house was lay'd,
> At moist *Capena* and th'old arches stay'd,
> Where mighty *Numa* and his Goddesse met,
> Whose sacred Grove and Fountaine are now let
> Withall her Temple-buildings to the Jewes,
> Whose hay and basket's all the stock they use.
> For ev'ry tree the peoples rent must pay:
> The poore Grove beggs, the muses turn'd away.   [pp. 21–22]

Three years later Stapleton changed only the last six lines, to:

> Where *Numa* every night his Goddesse found,
> Whose *Temple* and the *Woods* that still surround
> Her sacred *Fountaine* the *Jewes* hire; which they

Doe furnish with a *basket* and some *hay*.
For of each Tree the people's rent is made,
The Grove now begs, no more the Muse's shade.   [p. 34]

Why did Stapleton think he had made his translation better? Perhaps because the change from "mighty *Numa*" to "*Numa* every night" moves closer to the Latin ("nocturnae Numa"), and "furnish with a *basket* and some *hay*" (the 1647 compositor seems to have been well supplied with italic type) is more compact and returns a clearer rhyming sound than "Jewes"/"use" in the version of 1644, with its ugly sibilants. But if Stapleleton was trying to make his version more literal, it is hard to account for "no more the Muse's shade" in the last line; "the Muses turn'd away" of 1644 is closer to the original "eiectis . . . Camenis." Yet the 1647 version is better poetry—muses being especially fond of shade (see for example, Milton's *Paradise Lost* 3.27-28).

When we turn to the version of 1660, we find not only that the translation has been further revised, but also that it contains a new dedication (still to the Earl of Kingston), an added life of Juvenal, expanded notes, and attractive illustrations by leading artists and engravers, which make it one of the handsomest editions of a translation of Juvenal into English.[3] The title, like the format, has grown considerably, to *Mores Hominum. The Manners of Men, Described in Sixteen Satyrs, by Juvenal: As He Is Published in His Most Authentic Copy, Lately Printed by Command of the King of France. Whereunto Is Added the Invention of Seventeen Designes in Picture: With Argument to the Satyrs. And Also Explanations to the Designes in English and Latine. Together with a Large Comment, Clearing the Author in Every Place, wherein He Seemed Obscure, out of the Laws and Customes of the Romans, and the Latine and Greek Histories.*

The third satire now opens:

Though griev'd for my old friend's remove, I'm glad
He will at empty Cumae fix, and add
One Dweller to that Sybil's Town, the dore
To Baiae, sweet retirement's pleasant shore.

I would plant Prochyta your pretty Isle,
Ere dwell in our Suburra's goodly Pile:
For what so desolate, sad, horrid there,
As frights of fire, still falling houses here,
And thousand dangers which at Rome we dread,
Besides the Poets that in August read?
The Wagon, wherein all his house was lay'd,
At th'ancient Arc by moist Capena stay'd,
Where NUMA every night his Goddesse met
Where Temple, Spring, and Grove the People let
Now to the Jews, and all their stock to pay
Their Land-lords, is a Basket and some Hay;
Yet out of every tree the rent is made,
'Tis Beggars-bush, no more the Muses shade.

Since 1647, Stapleton seems have moved in two directions that much current theory of translation treats as antithetical; namely, attempting to approach more closely the literal meaning of the Latin and at the same time trying to write better poetry. Better poetry does not mean what would have seemed to Dryden and to Pope better couplets. Like most other earlier seventeenth-century translators, Stapleton ignores precision, closure, and balance, as we see from the opening three enjambments. He probably intended to match the flow of the Latin hexameter. The opening, "Though griev'd," is closer to the original "quamvis confusus," as is "Baiae" for "the Bath." "Prochyta"—the grammatically correct translation—for "Prochytas" shows a concern for accuracy. But other changes are harder to characterize. The paraphrase "your pretty Isle" may have been added to explain what Baiae was, or to set up a rhyme (since he'd lost the easy rhyme on "surpasse") with "Suburra's goodly Pile," a poeticism that I expect would have surprised Juvenal. "And thousand dangers which at Rome we dread" is slightly closer to the grammar of the Latin ("mille pericula saevae / urbis"), but the earlier "And thousand dangers this curste Towne must dreade" used more of Juvenal's vocabulary. "'Tis Beggars-bush," on the other hand, seems more vigorous and colloquial English than "The Grove now begs," although further from the Latin.

For those who like to see literary history on the march, the progress of Stapleton is a meandering route indeed. I suspect that as an amateur Stapleton was tinkering, not revising according to any clear idea of what a translation of Juvenal should be, and that as the titles of his translations indicate, he was more interested in conveying accurately what Juvenal has to say about manners and morals than in reproducing his literary technique.

[II]

In 1646 Henry Vaughan published *Poems with the Tenth Satyre of Iuvenal Englished* in London. For the young Vaughan, living in retirement in Wales, Horace might seem the more appropriate model, but as a Royalist Vaughan was hardly indifferent to the tumults of the great world, and found the tenth satire an appropriate comment on the ruin inordinate ambitions bring upon a nation. In a preface addressed "To all Ingenious Lovers of POESIE," Vaughan made it clear that he thought Juvenal had something to teach an England torn by civil conflict.

For the *Satyre*, it was of purpose borrowed, to feather some slower houres; And what you see here, is but the *Interest*, It is one of his, whose *Roman Pen* had as much true *Passion*, for the infirmities of that state, as we should have *Pitty*, to the distractions of our owne: Honest (I am sure) it is, and offensive cannot be, except it meet with such *Spirits* that will quarrell with *Antiquitie*, or purposely *Arraigne* themselves; These indeed may thinke, that they have slept out so many *Centuries* in this *Satyre*, and are now awaked: with, had it been still *Latine*, perhaps their Nap had been Everlasting.[4]

Satirists have been pretending since Horace's time that they write only to relieve the tedium of an idle hour, but the double and slightly contradictory assertion that a Roman satirist has an especial relevance for the present age, and that anyone who finds him offensive is equally bereft of classical accomplishments and good taste foreshadows the combative pose Alexander Pope was to take ninety years later.[5]

The translation of the tenth satire had a separate titlepage of its own containing that already familiar epigraph from Horace's *Ars poetica* warning us that Vaughan was going to take liberties with the original. Did these liberties include contemporary allusions? It has been suggested that Vaughan had in mind the attainder and execution of the Earl of Strafford when he translated Juvenal's account of the fall of Sejanus, though Vaughan's biographer suggests that some might doubt that Vaughan would have associated Strafford with so dubious a predecessor as Sejanus.[6] It does not follow that if Vaughan thought the fates of Sejanus and Strafford were parallel, he therefore thought that Strafford was a person similar to Sejanus, or for that matter that Charles I resembled Tiberius or parliament the Roman Senate. (Indeed, in the case of Strafford the roles were reversed; Parliament took the lead and King Charles I reluctantly acquiesed to the fall of his favorite.) Still, it is difficult to imagine a Royalist applying Juvenal's famous passage on Roman degeneracy to Englishmen.

> . . . iam pridem, ex quo suffragia nulli
> vendimus, effudit curas; nam qui dabat olim
> imperium fasces legiones omnia, nunc se
> continet atque duas tantum res anxius optat
> panem et circenses . . .   [77–81]

[It has now been a long time since we sold votes, (the Roman populace) has given up its cares, what once bestowed military and civil authority, legions, and everything, now restrains itself and is concerned about only two things, bread and circuses.]

It is equally difficult to think of a loyal subject applying Vaughan's rendering to England.

> But Rome is now growne wise, & since that she
> Her Suffrages, and ancient Libertie,
> Lost in a Monarchs name; she takes no care
> For Favourite, or Prince; nor will she share
> Their fickle glories, though in *Cato's* dayes
> She rul'd whole States & Armies with her voice,
> Of all the honours now within her walls,
> She only doats on Playes, and Festivalls.   [141–47]

Surely "ancient Libertie, / Lost in a Monarchs name" and the change from bread and circuses to "Playes, and Festivalls" sound more like something a Roundhead would write. Puritans detested the theatre and regarded a holiday as a Popish abomination and as a clog on trade. On purely internal evidence one might well try to claim the passage for Milton.[7]

As this sample shows, like the earlier Biddle and the later Dryden, Vaughan is an expansive translator, but unlike Biddle and Dryden, he adds details without making Juvenal's meaning much clearer. Where Juvenal disguises a proper name in a paraphrase, Vaughan often does too. An early section of the tenth satire gives us a good chance to assess Vaughan's technique. Juvenal begins by remarking that the common prayer heard in the temples is for wealth; then he appeals to the authority of a pair of ancient philosophers, neither of whose works survive.

iamne igitur laudas quod de sapientibus alter
ridebat, quotiens a limine moverat unum
protuleratque pedem, flebat contrarius auctor?
sed facilis cuivis rigidi censura cachinni:
mirandum est unde ille oculis suffecerit umor.
perpetuo risu pulmonem agitare solebat
Democritus, quamquam non essent urbibus illis
praetextae trabeae fasces lectica tribunal;
quid si vidisset praetorem curribus altis
extantem et medii sublimem pulvere circi
in tunica Jovis et pictae Sarrana ferentem
ex umeris aulaea togae magnaeque coronae
tantum orbem, quanto cervix non sufficit ulla?
quippe tenet sudans hanc publicus et, sibi consul
ne placeat, curru servus portatur eodem.   [28-42]

[Do you not, then, now praise that at which one of the two wisemen used to laugh, whenever he stepped out of his house, at which the other wiseman wept? But the censure of a stiff bellylaugh comes easily to anybody: the marvel is how enough liquid supplied the eyes. Democritus was accustomed to shake his sides with continuous laughing, although in his cities there were no senatorial gowns, robes of state, emblems of

the magistrate's authority, palanquins, and tribunal: what if he were to
see a praetor standing in his high car above the dust in the middle of the
circus in the tunic of Jupiter and bearing the Tyrian tapestry of an
embroidered toga from his shoulders and the entire circle of a great
crown, too heavy for any neck? Indeed, a sweating public slave holds it,
and lest the consul be pleased with himself, he is carried in the same
chariot.]

This kind of passage sets one of the hardest tests that a translator
can face. With notes it is easy enough to explain what Juvenal is
saying, but his allusions are very cryptic. The weeping philosopher, Heraclitus, is never named, and Juvenal keeps us waiting for
seven verses before telling us the laughing philosopher was
Democritus. The costumes and insignia of Roman political ranks
and offices have no English equivalents and can only be rendered
by transliterations, paraphrases, or arcane expressions. As is often
the case, Juvenal's sudden jumps from topic to topic, from the
early philosophers to the pomp of contemporary Rome, leave
Vaughan's leisurely couplets ambling behind.

> Blam'st thou the Sages then? because the one
> Would still be laughing, when he would be gone
> From his owne doore, the other cryed to see
> His times addicted to such vanity?
> Smiles are an easie purchase, but to weep
> Is a hard act, for teares are fetch'd more deep;
> *Democritus* his nimble Lungs would tyre
> With constant laughter, and yet keep entire
> His stocke of mirth, for ev'ry object was
> Addition to his store; though then (Alas!)
> Sedans, and Litters, and our Senat Gownes,
> With Robes of honour, fasces, and the frownes
> Of unbrib'd Tribunes were not seene; but had
> He lived to see our *Roman Praetor* clad
> In *Joves* owne mantle, seated on his high
> Embroyder'd Chariot 'midst the dust and Crie
> Of the large Theatre, loaden with a Crowne
> Which scarse he could support, (for it would downe,
> But that his servant props it) and close by
> His page a witnes to his vanitie.   [45-64]

But despite the wordiness and some obvious expedients for rhyme ("Alas!" "vanity" rhyming with "see" and "vanitie" with "by"), Vaughan's couplets move energetically. Sometimes Vaughan paraphrases ("Senat Gownes," "Robes of honour"), sometimes transliterates ("fasces," "*Praetor*"), and sometimes adds his own comments, as in "frownes / Of unbrib'd Tribunes were not seene" for "tribunal." A doublet such as "Sedans, and Litters" for "lectica" may not be a sign of incompetence or the need for three more syllables; as we have seen with Biddle, seventeenth-century writers liked pleonasms. "Embroyder'd Chariot" is probably a bold attempt at a transferred epithet rather than a mistranslation, but "His page a witnes to his vanitie" suggests that Vaughan meant a different servant from the slave who propped up the praetor's crown.

Juvenal continued:

da nunc et volucrem, sceptro quae surgit eburno,
illinc cornicines, hinc praecedentia longi
agminis officia et niveos ad frena Quirites,
defossa in loculos quos sportula fecit amicos.
tum quoque materiam risus invenit ad omnis
occursus hominum, cuius prudentia monstrat
summos posse viros et magna exempla daturos
vervecum in patria crassoque sub aere nasci.
ridebat curas nec non et gaudia volgi,
interdum et lacrimas, cum Fortunae ipse minaci
mandaret laqueum mediumque ostenderet unguem.   [43-54]

[And now add the eagle, which rises from the ivory scepter, on the far side are trumpeters, on the near side a long train of clients and Roman citizens in snow-white togas, friends purchased by the meal tickets hidden in their cashboxes. Then too he found it a laughing matter whenever people met; his prudence shows that the greatest men and best examples can arise in a country of blockheads (literally, wethers) and under thick skies. He laughed at the cares and at the joys of the common folk and also at their tears, yet he told Fortune to get a noose when she threatened him and stuck out his middle finger.]

Like Juvenal's other references to philosophers, this one is a curious combination of admiration and contempt. While regarding Democritus, like most philosophers, as a crank and a faddest— and no doubt as a foreigner as well—Juvenal endorses his scorn for human folly. So did Vaughan, who translates:

To these his Scepter, and his Eagle adde
His Trumpets, Officers, and servants clad
In white, and purple; with the rest that day,
He hir'd to triumph for his bread, and pay;
Had he these studied, sumptuous follies seene,
'Tis thought his wanton, and effusive spleen
Had kill'd the Abderite, though in that age
(When pride & greatnes had not swell'd the stage
So high as ours) his harmles, and just mirth
From ev'ry object had a suddaine birth;
Nor wast alone their avarice, or pride,
Their triumphs, or their cares he did deride;
Their vaine contentions, or ridiculous feares;
But even their very poverty, and teares.
He would at fortunes threats as freely smile
As others mourne; nor was it to beguile
His crafty passions; but this habit he
By nature had, and grave Philosophie.
He knew their idle and superfluous vowes,
And sacrifice, which such wrong zeale bestowes,
Were mere Incendiaries; and that the gods
Not pleas'd therewith, would ever be at ods;
Yet to no other aire, nor better place
Ow'd he his birth, then the cold, homely *Thrace;*
Which shewes a man may be both wise, & good,
Without the brags of fortune, or his bloud.   [65-90]

A modern critic has remarked, "The most obvious effect of Vaughan's method of translating is the difficulty it poses in determining his share in the poem. Sometimes lines that seem clear additions to the original turn out upon close inspection to be only loose paraphrases, at other points, Vaughan can nearly bury from sight a particular attitude of his own in a section of the poem that seems otherwise faithful to Juvenal."[8] Here, for example, "idle and superfluous vowes" may appear to be Vaughan's inserted opinion, but the wording could be seen as anticipating Juvenal's "supervacua" in verse 54. "In white, and purple" for Juvenal's "nivea" seems to be padding, and misleading padding at that, unless suggested by "praetextae" in verse 35, which were togas with purple borders. Some details that certainly are Vaughan's inventions, such as "'Tis thought his wanton, and effusive spleene / Had kill'd the Abderite," do not offer any obvious reason for Vaughan's having added them. Maybe he wanted to show that he knew Democritus' birthplace as he later makes clear that Thrace was the land noted (at least among the Athenians) for its heavy air and consequently the thick wits of its inhabitants. Yet Vaughan tries to paint a more dignified picture of Democritus, adding that his laughter was not "to beguile / His crafty passions; but this habit he / By nature had, and grave Philosophie." Vaughan probably was trying to steer the reader by supplying whatever he thought literal translation would omit, whether by incorporating material that would normally be found in glosses, by emphasizing (and sometimes perhaps changing) the tone of the original, and by adding *sententiae* of his own, some of which may have been influenced by recent political events.

Today we think of Vaughan as a "metaphysical" religious poet, a follower of George Herbert, and although he translated Juvenal's tenth satire at least a couple of years before his conversion, one is naturally curious to see what he made of the Roman satirist's famous conclusion.

Nil ergo optabunt homines? si consilium vis,
permittes ipsis expendere numinibus quid
conveniat nobis rebusque sit utile nostris.
nam pro iucundis aptissima quaeque dabunt di:
carior est illis homo quam sibi. nos animorum
inpulsu et caeca magnaque cupidine ducti
coniugium petimus partumque uxoris, at illis
notum qui pueri qualisque futura sit uxor.

ut tamen et poscas aliquid voveasque sacellis
exta et candiduli divina tomacula porci,
orandum est ut sit mens sana in corpore sano.
fortem posce animum mortis terrore carentem,
qui spatium vitae extremum inter munera ponat
naturae, qui ferre queat quoscumque labores,
nesciat irasci, cupiat nihil et potiores
Herculis aerumnas credat saevosque labores
et Venere et cenis et plumna Sardanapalli.
monstro quod ipse tibi possis dare; semita certe
tranquillae per virtutem patet unica vitae.
nullum numen habes, si sit prudentia: nos te,
nos facimus, Fortuna, deam caeloque locamus.   [346-66]

[Shall men then pray for nothing? If you want advice, leave it to the gods themselves to provide what is appropriate for us and useful to our condition. For the gods give whatever is most suitable for happy persons: a man is dearer to them than he is to himself. We, led by irrational impulse and blind and great desire, seek a wife and the offspring of a wife, but to the gods is known what sort of children and what kind of wife they will be. Yet so that you might ask for something and vow entrails at the shrines and divine little sausages of a white piglet, pray that a sound mind be in a sound body. Ask for a brave mind that lacks fear of death and regards length of life least among the gifts of nature, a mind which is able to bear all kinds of hardships, which does not know how to be angry, desires nothing, and prefers the tasks and terrible labors of Hercules to the sexual pleasures and dinners and featherbeds of Sardanapalus. I prescribe what you yourself can give to yourself; surely the one secure path to a quiet life lies through virtue. If there be prudence, Fortune, you have no divinity: we, we make you a goddess and put you in heaven.]

It has been remarked that the blank verse of Samuel Johnson's tragedy *Irene* reads as if it were written in unrhymed heroic couplets; Vaughan's enjambed couplets are a bit like rhymed blank verse.

What then should man pray for? what is't that he
Can beg of Heaven, without Impiety?

Take my advice: first to the Gods commit
All cares; for they things competent, and fit
For us foresee; besides man is more deare
To them, then to himselfe: we blindly here
Led by the world, and lust, in vaine assay
To get us portions, wives, and sonnes; but they
Already know all that we can intend,
And of our Childrens Children see the end.
   Yet that thou may'st have something to commend
With thankes unto the Gods for what they send;
Pray for a wise, and knowing soule; a sad
Discreet, true valour, that will scorne to adde
A needless horrour to thy death; that knowes
'Tis but a debt which man to nature owes;
That starts not at misfortunes, that can sway,
And keep all passions under locke and key;
That covets nothing, wrongs none, preferres
An honest want before rich injurers;
All thus thou hast within thy selfe, and may
Be made thy owne, if thou wilt take the way;
What boots the worlds wild, loose applause? what can
Frail, perillous honours adde unto a man?
What length of years, wealth, or a rich faire wife?
Vertue alone can make a happy life.
To a wise man nought comes amisse: but we
Fortune adore, and make our Deity.   [524-51]

Some modern readers are uncomfortable with Juvenal's contemptuous attitude toward religious offerings.[9] Probably seventeenth-century Christian readers felt otherwise; Juvenal was talking,
after all, about pagan prayer to deities who were either fictitious
or diabolical. Juvenal's expression "voveas" implies a kind of
bribe—in Roman religion one offered a sacrifice with the expectation that the deity would do something favorable in return.
Vaughan's worshipper offers "thankes" for grace already bestowed
instead. And the *sententia* to pray for a sound mind in a healthy
body disappears to become the injunction to pray for "a wise, and
knowing soule" instead. That it will "scorne to adde / A needless

horrour" to death may be a particularly Christian change, because despite Christ's victory over death, death remains an evil and a consequence of sin to be feared; the Stoic wiseman regards death with *apathia*, if not as a gift of nature, which was one common gloss on verse 358. Juvenal's rhetorical *exempla*, Hercules and Sardanapalus, have been banished as well, in favor of a Christian attitude toward this world's goods and their possessors. According to the usual chronology, Henry Vaughan's translation of the tenth satire of Juvenal appeared two years before his younger brother William's death, which caused Henry to turn seriously to religion. Yet by 1646 Vaughan was already so pious that he came closer than any other seventeenth-century translator to making a Christian convert of Juvenal.

[III]

When W. H. Auden characterized Horatians as "political idiots,"[10] I do not think he meant that Horace's admirers were too defective mentally to be allowed to vote, but that Auden was using "idiot" in the sense of the Greek *idiotēs* to designate a private citizen who took no part in the government of the polis. So understood, the term well fits John Smith, translator of a selection from Horace entitled *The Lyrick Poet: Odes and Satyres* (1649), for he seems to have done nothing to gain an entry in standard biographical reference works. Each of Horace's poems he translated is dedicated to a specific person, some identified as relatives of Smith's. None of them appears in the *Dictionary of National Biography*, except Edward Heveningham, the regicide judge, so Smith may have been a Roundhead. Whatever his politics, Smith's poetry is as prosaic as his name. Smith translated five of Horace's satires, 1.1; 1.3; 1.8; 1.9; and 2.6. In none of them does much of Smith come through in English. He adds no details or glosses and appears content to arrange a literal English version into couplets. But modest and self-effacing translators do better to avoid Horace. When Horace starts being clever, Smith finds himself out of his depth. The eighth satire of the first book is one of Horace's funniest satires, though not one that the Victorians found very elevating. Its target is Canidia, a witch whom the commentators identified with a cosmetics salesperson who was supposed to have had an affair with Horace. It must have ended badly, for in addition to this satire Horace also wrote two epodes against her.[11] Here the speaker is a scarecrow, a wooden statue of Priapus standing in the garden of Maecenas, who describes how one night he saw Canidia and another witch, Sagana, summoning ghosts. The Priapus was so frightened by the eerie spectacle that he— well, let Horace tell it.

. . . Hecaten vocat altera, saevam
altera Tisiphonen: serpentes atque videres
infernas errare canes Lunam rubentem,
ne foret his testis, post magna latere sepulcra.
mentior at siquid, merdis caput inquiner albis
corvorum atque in me veniat mictum atque cacatum
Iulius et fragilis Pediatia furque Voranus.
singula quid memorem, quo pacto alterna loquentes
umbrae cum Sagana resonarint triste et acutum
utque lupi barbam variae cum dente colubrae
abdiderint furtim terris et imagine cerea
largior arserit ignis et ut non testis inultus
horruerim voces furiarum et facta duarum?
nam, displosa sonat quantum vesica, pepedi
diffissa nate ficus; at illae currere in urbem.
Canidiae dentis, altum Saganae caliendrum
excidere atque herbas atque incantata lacertis
vincula cum magno risuque iocoque videres.   [33-50]

[One calls Hecate, the other fierce Tisiphone: you would have seen serpents and hounds of hell wandering and the moon blushing, and hiding behind the great tombs so as not to witness these things. If I am lying at all, let my head be fouled with the white droppings of crows and let Julius and frail Pediatia and the thief Voranus piss and shit on me. Why should I recite the details, how the shades speaking in turn with Sagana resounded sad and shrill as they buried secretly in the earth the beard of a wolf with the tooth of a spotted snake and the fire flared from a waxen image and how I, a soon-to-be-avenged witness, was horrified by the voices and deeds of the two furies? For, loud as a pig's bladder bursting, I farted from my cracked figwood buttocks; but they ran into the city. You would have seen Canidia lose her false teeth and Sagana her big wig as well as the herbs and the magic amulets bound to their arms, as you enjoyed a big laugh and a joke.]

Smith leans on Horace for his vocabulary and for his syntax as well. (Notice how "with great mirth and laughter" echoes the Latin ablative.)

Th'one *Hecate* call, th'other *Tisephone;*
Hels-dogs and Serpents to stray you may see
And the Moon blushing, lest by these espied
And witnesse made, behinde the graves did hide.
And if I lie, I wish that now my head
May with white-dung of Crowes be covered;
Julius, Pedatus, Voranus the scum,
On me to pisse and th'other thing may come.
Why should I reckon all? how in their course
The Ghost with *Sagana* sound shrill and hoarse?
And how close in the earth they had interr'd
With tooth of spotted snake, and old woolfs beard,
With th' waxen Image how the fire did flame,
And how I seeing all revenged came.
How I the voice of Furies silenc'd quite,
And the two witches facts did sore affright.
And I *Priapus* such a crack out thrust
As sounded like a bladder when it's burst.
But these two startled ran into the Towne,
Canidias teeth, and *Saganas* curls fell down,
When with great mirth and laughter you might spie
Hearbs & charm'd strings falne from theire own armes to lie.
[p. 150]

Some things that sound odd to us would not bother a seventeenth-century reader; "fact" (in the sense of "deed") appears to be a Latinism, however, "evil deed" or "crime" was its usual sense then (as in the legal phrase "accessory after the fact"). But "th'other thing" for "cacatum" belongs in the nursery. Smith's "such a crack out thrust" is much more refined than Horace's "pepedi" and conveys no comic climax. Smith was not trying to translate all the satires, so if he found the coarse humor of the eighth satire distasteful why did he bother with it at all? Smith is no Barksted, who nearly achieves the Platonic ideal of the bad translator; he is simply dull, and dullness is fatal when attempting Horace, who depends so much on placing every word cleverly and accurately.[12] Juvenal's style and subjects are sensational enough to survive a fairly literal rendering. But for Horatian effects that do not travel well the translator has to supply amusing ingredients of his own.[13]

[IV]

Richard Fanshawe was a "political idiot" only by constraint. He was, perhaps, the last of those brilliant Renaissance amateurs who excelled both as poets and as statesmen. A Royalist, he was captured after the battle of Worcester and in September 1651 imprisoned at Whitehall. The next year his *Selected Parts of Horace, Prince of Lyricks; and of All the Latin Poets the Fullest Fraught with Excellent Morality* appeared, which suggests how he had passed the time in jail. Fanshawe was already an accomplished translator. His versions of Guarini's *Il Pastor Fido* (in couplets) and of the fourth book of the *Aeneid* (into Spenserian stanzas) had appeared in 1647. In 1655 he would publish a translation of the national epic of Portugal, Camoens's *Lusiads*, using the original *ottava rima*, which is still unsurpassed. Appropriately, after the Restoration Charles II sent him to Lisbon as his ambassador. Most of the selections from Horace are from the odes as the title suggests, but Fanshawe included renderings of three of the satires, 1.6; 2.1; and 2.6 (as well as four of the epistles), all into heroic couplets. A Latin text taken from John Bond's school edition occupies each verso, so the educated reader could easily compare Fanshawe's version to the original.[14]

In the sixth satire of the first book Horace defends his character and upbringing against detractors who saw him as an upstart and a parvenu. It is true, Horace answers, that his father was a freedman, but he provided Horace with a first-rate education. Horace disowns any political or social ambitions and closes the satire with a description of how quietly he passes his days.

> ... quacumque libido est,
> incedo solus, percontor quanti holus ac far,
> fallacem circum vespertinumque pererro
> saepe forum, adsisto divinis, inde domum me
> ad porri et ciceris refero laganique catinum;
> cena ministratur pueris tribus et lapis albus
> pocula cum cyantho duo sustinet, adstat echinus
> vilis, cum patera guttus, Campana supellex.
> deinde eo dormitum, non sollicitus, mihi quod cras
> surgendum sit mane, obeundus Marsya, qui se
> voltum ferre negat Noviorum posse minoris.
> ad quartam iaceo; post hanc vagor aut ego lecto
> aut scripto quod me tacitum iuvet unguor olivo,
> non quo fraudatis inmundus Natta lucernis.
> ast ubi me fessum sol acrior ire lavatum
> admonuit, fugio rabiosi tempora signi.
> pransus non avide, quantum interpellet inani
> ventre diem durare, domesticus otior. haec est
> vita solutorum misera ambitione gravique;
> his me consolor victurum suavius ac si
> quaestor avus pater atque meus patruusque fuisset.   [111-31]

[I stroll alone wherever I want to, I enquire about the price of vegetables and flour, often I wander about the deceitful Forum in the evening, I visit the temples, then I return home to a platter of leeks or chickpeas or pancakes; dinner is served by three servants and my white stone table bears a cup with two dippers; there is a cheap salt cellar, and a flask next to a bowl, Campana ware. Then I sleep, not worried that when morning comes I shall have to go see Marsyas, who says that he cannot bear the face of the younger Novius. Till ten I lie in bed; afterwards I wander about or after reading or writing something that pleases me, I am quietly annointed with olive oil, not the sort that dirty Natta stole from lamps. But when a fierce sun suggests it to me, I go to the baths, I flee the hottest days. Having lunched lightly, on as much as serves to pass the day without an empty stomach, I stay home at leisure. This is the life of those free from wretched and pressing ambition; with these things I console myself that I live better than if a quaestor had been my grandfather and my father and my uncle.]

Foreign food and ancient nobodies challenge any translator. Marsyas was supposed to have been attendant of Bacchus; his statue stood in the Forum, and Horace pretends to believe that he was sculpted with his arm upraised because he cannot stand the sight of the younger of the Novii, a pair of usurers. We know nothing about Natta. Apparently he was a miser so mean that he had himself rubbed down with lamp oil, which given the Romans' obsession with skin care, was niggardly indeed. Fanshawe adds little, but there are some subtle changes.

> ... Where e're I list I go,
> Alone, the price of Broath, and Barley know;
> Crow'd in at every *Sight*, walk late in *Rome:*
> Visit the *Temple* with a Prayer: Then home
> To my Leek-Pottage & Chich-pease. Three boyes
> Serve in my supper: Whom to counterpoyse
> One Bowle, two Beakers on a broad white slate,
> A Pitcher with two Ears (*Campanian* plate.)
> Then do I go to sleep: securely do't,
> Being next morning to attend no suite
> In the *Great-Hall* (where *Marsya* doth look,
> As if lowd *Novio*'s Face he could not brooke)
> I lie till Four. Then walk, or read a while;
> Or write, to please my self. Noint me with oil;
> (Not such as *Natta* pawes himself withall,
> Robbing the Lamps). When neer his Vertical
> The hotter Sun invites us to a Bath
> For our tir'd Limbs, I fly the Dog-Stars wrath,
> Having din'd onely so much as may stay
> My Appetite: Loiter at home all Day.
> These are my Solaces: this is the life
> Of Men that shun ambition, run from strife.
> Lighter, then if I soar'd on *Glorie*'s wing,
> *The Nephew, Son, and Grand-Son to a King.*   [p. 75]

At first sight Fanshawe seems very free. But some glosses have crept in from Bond's Latin text. Fanshawe's Horace, instead of being relieved that he does not have to face a usurious creditor, is not required to answer a lawsuit instead, because Bond described the younger Novius (Fanshawe's original text reads "Nomio's," perhaps based on Bond's "Numio," which may be a typographical error) as an "improbissimus litigator" and "the Dog-stars wrath" may owe something to Bond's gloss on "rabiosi tempora signi" as "Caniculus." "King" for "quaestor" seems an odd change, since quaestor was the lowest office in the Roman *cursus honorum*. Maybe Fanshawe assumed that as Horace addressed this satire to Maecenas, descended from Etruscan kings, the change would be fitting. "Broath, and Barley" instead of Horace's "holus ac far" quietly changes Horace's Mediterranean diet to something more congenial to English taste.

Fanshawe's verse technique belongs to the new era. Strong caesuras and enjambments weave clearly articulated couplets together to make the rhymes less obtrusive, as fits the pedestrian style. Two single-couplet periods, the first unbalanced and the second stopped, round off the poem nicely.

As we shall see, the line between a free translation and an Imitation is a difficult one to draw. Fanshawe's version of the sixth satire of the second book adds anachronistic details without changing the setting. Horace says he has known Maecenas for nearly eight years, and though they never talk politics, everybody thinks Horace is privy to official secrets.

septimus octavo propior iam fugerit annus,
ex quo Maecenas me coepit habere suorum
in numero, dumtaxat ad hoc, quem tollere raeda
vellet iter faciens et cui concredere nugas
hoc genus: "hora quota est?" "Thraex est Gallina Syro par?"
"matutina parum cautos iam frigora mordent,"
et quae rimosa bene deponuntur in aure.
per totum hoc tempus subiectior in diem et horam
invidiae noster. ludos spectaverat, una
luserat in campo: "fortunae filius" omnes.
frigidus a rostris manat per compita rumor:
quicumque obvius est, me consulit: "o bone—nam te
scire, deos quoniam propius contingis oportet—,
numquid de Dacis audisti?" "nil equidem.". . .   [40-53]

[The seventh—more nearly the eighth—year has flown past, from when Maecenas began to include me in the number of his friends, to this extent, that when making a journey he would take me with him in his carriage and entrust to me trifles of this kind: "What time is it?" "Is the Thracian gamecock (the nickname of a gladiator) a match for the Syrian?" "These morning chills will bite the careless," and the kinds of things that are deposited in a leaky ear. During all this time at every day and hour I am subjected to envy. After we've watched the games together or played on the Campus, everybody calls me "Fortune's child." A chilling rumor leaks from the speaker's platform through the cross-roads. Whoever encounters me consults me: "My dear fellow—you ought to know because you're in close touch with the top people—have you heard anything about the Dacians?" (The Romans feared that the Dacians would attack while they were preoccupied in Egypt with Antony and Cleopatra.) "Nothing indeed."]

Watching Fanshawe adapt Horace's essentially Roman substance to English is like seeing a chef concocting an exotic dish from native ingredients.

> ... 'Tis now
> A seven years past, *Maecenas* doth allow
> Me of his family, only t'advise
> Whom he should take into his Coach in Journeys.
> To whom commit his Meddals: What's a Clock?
> Which Fencer will beat (think'st thou) or which Cock?
> 'Tis a hard Frost: wil't bear another Coat?
> With such like trifles as are safely put
> In Leaking Ears. This Prentiship have I
> Serv'd under Envy's lash, more and more daily.
> *Our Friend bowl'd with* Maecenas *th'other day:*
> I, and they sate together at the Play:
> (*Some men have Fortune!*) Blows there through the street
> A bleak news from the Change? straight all I meet;
> *Good man: (for thou being neere the Gods must know)*
> *Do'st hear ought of the Dacians?* In sooth, No.   [pp. 80-81]

The questioner's anxiety about the Dacians firmly anchors us in ancient Rome. But the Latin seems to have resonated in Fanshawe's mind to suggest distinctly English touches. Horace's "nugas" suggests "Meddals"—connoting at the time *trinkets*. The gladiator nicknamed "Gallina" reminds Fanshawe of cockfighting, playing (ball, I assume) in the Campus suggests bowling, and the *ludi*, which could be theatrical or gladiatorial shows, the theatre. "Change" for the "rostra"—the platform in the Forum from which announcements were made, could be a deliberate modernizing touch, or it could simply be Fanshawe's notion of the most accurate English translation, as I suspect "What's a Clock?", would have been for "hora quota est?"

Whether Fanshawe was consciously modernizing or not, at mid-century he had substantially realized the two great achievements of Restoration translators of Roman satire. The first was a mastery of couplet technique to reconcile a clearly defined verse structure with a syntax reasonably close to conversational English. The second was to find a style and vocabulary that would allow a Roman satirist to speak contemporary English without sounding like a foreigner, while at the same time avoiding howling anachronisms. As we shall see in the following chapters, it was to be a good many years before most later translators had assimilated Fanshawe's technique.

Early Restoration Adaptations

[I]

It would make the literary historian's task easier if Restoration adaptations of Roman satire showed a clear line of development culminating in the Dryden translation of 1692, or if at least they fell into easily defined categories. One scholar has indeed divided Restoration translators into "the 'dominant' modern school," and those who employed "older, more scholarly, conservative methods."[1] But as we have seen, many "older" translators were anything but "conservative"; the unfortunate Barksted perhaps setting the record. We might better regard translations after 1660 as a series of experiments testing various methods, all of which were, finally, available to Dryden and his assistants.

The Poems of Horace, Consisting of Odes, Satyres, and Epistles, Rendred in English Verse by Several Persons (1666), is largely the work of Alexander Brome. He started with Fanshawe's translations and added new ones, by himself and others, to provide a complete version of Horace in English. Only the satires need concern us here. Brome did not learn much about technique from Fanshawe. His couplets are sprawling and shapeless, even though in the introduction to the volume he praised Edmund Waller and Sir John Denham and looked forward to what improved versification could accomplish. Perhaps Brome was simply incompetent, or he may have made the same mistake as John Smith, believing that the Horatian *sermo pedestris* ought to sound "pedestrian" in English. Of course, Horace can be quite direct and prosaic, as in the second satire of the first book, where he reproves the fastidious adulterer who only fancies women of the upper classes, and accepts being teased and frustrated as part of the fun.

nonne, cupidinibus statuat natura modum quem,
quid latura sibi, quid sit dolitura negatum,
quaerere plus prodest et inane abscindere soldo?
num, tibi cum fauces urit sitis, aurea quaeris
pocula? num esuriens fastidis omnia praeter
pavonem rhombumque? tument tibi cum inguina, num, si
ancilla aut verna est praesto puer, impetus in quem
continuo fiat, malis tentigine rumpi?
non ego; namque parabilem amo venerem facilemque.   [111–18]

[Is it not more profitable to seek the mean that nature has established for our desires, what she can bear to be deprived of, and what she cannot do without, and to separate the illusory from the real? For when your throat burns with thirst, do you ask for a golden cup? When you are hungry do you turn your nose up at everything but peacock and turbot? When your organ swells, if there is a slave girl or boy handy in whom you can stick it straightway, would you rather burst from the pressure instead? Not I: For I like quick and easy sex.]

Horace's moral is essentially Epicurean, that for men extramarital sex—whether heterosexual or homosexual—is a harmless amusement so long as it does not involve excessive trouble or expense that would interfere with family and civic obligations, and therefore the libido should be satisfied with the least possible fuss.[2] In seventeenth-century England official Christian standards were quite different and one is eager to see what Brome makes of such alien sentiments.

When thou art *thirsty* must thou onely drink
Out of a Golden *goblet*? or dost think
All *meat* is loathsome, when thou'rt *hungry* grown,
But *Turbet*, or the *Pheasant* poult alone?
   So when thy *amorous* flames grow strong and high,
Wilt thou not take the next thou canst come by?
Be't *Kitchin* wench, or *Scullion* boy; or else
Wouldst have that burst, which so exreamly swells?

I'm of another humour, for to me
That *girl* is best, that's easiest, and she
That I can soonest come at . . .   [pp. 196-97]

Brome keeps the same fish but alters the fowl. (We recall from
Juvenal that peacock was lethal anyway.) Quite literal too is
turning the "ancilla" and "verna . . . puer" into the "*Kitchin*
wench" and "*Scullion* boy"—the casual assumption that the
audience is bisexual fits the ancient Romans much better than
seventeen-century Englishmen, if we except those with the tastes
satirists attributed to Lord Rochester. Yet the flavor of the
translation is different; whatever liberties a seventeenth- or eighteenth-century master might be accustomed to take with his
servants (we have the evidence of Defoe and Richardson), they
were surely not slaves whose sexual favors were available at the
master's whim. And the substitution of "*girl*" (given the unpredic-
tability of seventeenth-century printers, I would not venture a
guess as to whether the italics are emphatic or not) for Horace's
"venerem" makes Horace sound more heterosexual than he really
was; *venus* can refer to relationships with either sex. Of course
euphemisms such as "amorous flames" for "inguina" were the rule
for sexually explicit passages in English, though the metaphor fits
erotic poetry (one thinks of Sappho's famous *lepton pur*) better
than the unabashed Horatian *sermo*.

Thomas Flatman's translation of the fourth satire of the second
book,[3] which appears in the same volume, is more difficult to
classify as either literal or free. This satire is a dialogue between
Horace and a gourmet named Catius, a talking cookbook. According to scholars, who say the poem may be a satire on the
Epicureans, the humor lies in the reverence Catius displays
towards gastronomy. Personally, I have never found the poem
funny, perhaps because most of Catius' favorite dishes are so
revolting. A typical example is Catius' recipe for an appetite
ruined by too much drinking.

tostis marcentem squillis recreabis et Afra
potorem coclea; nam lactuca innatat acri

post vinum stomacho; perna magis et magis hillis
flagitat inmorsus refici, quin omnia malit
quaecumque inmundis fervent allata popinis.　　　　[58-62]

[You will restore a jaded appetite with fried shrimps and a soup of
African snails; for after wine, lettuce floats on a sour stomach; which
after being bitten burns to be refreshed with more ham and more
sausages, even the kind of slop dished out at filthy cookshops.]

Flatman transformed the passage to read:

"An o're charg'd stomach roasted *Shrimps* will ease.
"The cure by *Lettice* is worse then the disease.
"To quicken appetite it will behove ye
"To feed courageously on good *Anchovie.*
"*Westphalia Hamm,* and the *Bolognia* sausage;
"For second or third course will clear a passage,
"But *Lettice* after meals! Fie on't! the Glutton
"Had better feed up on *Ram-alley-Mutton.*"　　　　[p. 269]

Flatman's dishes are much the same as Horace's, but does adding
"Westphalia," "Bolognia," and "Ram-alley" cross the line between
free translation and Imitation? Without relying on any obvious
principle, I think not. Here, although Horace never heard of
Westphalia or Ram-alley, the names seem generic, not local, like
Fanshawe's translation of the Forum as " 'Change."

In Thomas Sprat's versions of the ninth satire of the first book,
and of the first part of the sixth satire of the second book, and the
completion of the latter by Abraham Cowley, we have the first
full-scale Imitations of a classical satirist.[4] One critic has main-
tained that these versions are merely translations, arguing that
"modernization is restricted to the substitution of a few details
(e.g., London for Rome)," and that "the poems remain essentially
Roman."[5] But can we say that the poem "remain[s] essentially
Roman" when Sprat puts his friend Cowley into his version? In
the original, Horace—the bore stuck to him like a limpet—
encounters his friend Fuscus Aristius. Horace tries to get rid of
his tormentor by making Fuscus pretend to have some confiden-

tial information for Horace. But the waggish Fuscus finds Horace's plight amusing and invents a preposterous excuse for having to leave at once.

> ... haec dum agit, ecce
> Fuscus Aristius occurrit, mihi carus et illum
> qui pulcre nosset. consistimus. "unde venis et
> quo tendis?" rogat et respondet. vellere coepi
> et pressare manu lentissima bracchia, nutans,
> distorquens oculos, ut me eriperet. male salsus
> ridens dissimulare; meum iecur urere bilis.
> "certe nescio quid secreto velle loqui te
> aiebas mecum." "memini bene, sed meliore
> tempore dicam; hodie tricesima sabbata: vin tu
> curtis Iudaeis oppedere?" "nulla mihi" inquam
> "relligio est." "at mi: sum paulo infirmior, unus
> multorum. ignosces; alias loquar." huncine solem
> tam nigrum surrexe mihi! fugit inprobus ac me
> sub cultro linquit. ...   [60-74]

[While he does this, behold Fuscus Aristius arrives, a dear friend who recognizes the bore very well. We stop. He questions me and asks, "Where are you coming from and where are you going?" I start grab at him and to catch hold of his unresponsive arms, nodding and rolling my eyes about, so he would rescue me. But the wretch laughs and pretends not to understand. My liver burns with bile. "Surely you wanted to talk to me about some hush-hush I-don't-know what." "I recall it well, but I'll tell you at a more appropriate time. Today is the Thirtieth Sabbath: do you want to offend the circumcised Jews?" "Religion is nothing to me." "But it is to me; I'm one of the weaker brethren, one of many. Excuse me; I'll tell you later." That such a dark day should befall me! The rogue takes off and leaves me under the knife.]

Cowley equally enjoys watching his friend thrash about in the bore's toils.

While he did thus run on, who should we meet
But my friend *C[owley]* passing cross the street.
C[owley] straight found what kind of man he was,

Nor to see through him, need he his glass:
So when the usual *complements* were past,
I trod on's toes, and softly him imbrac't;
I winkt, and shrug'd, and many signes I gave,
Which silently did his assistance crave:
But my *unmerciful* malitious friend,
Seem'd not to understand what I intend,
Enjoy'd my misery, and smil'd to see
What thin small *Plots* I made to be set free.
Dear friend! d'ye remember who last night
Did us to dine with him to day invite?
I well rem[em]ber it, but yet in troth
I have no mind to go, for I am loth
To break a fasting day, as we shall there,
There's nought I have a dispensation here.
I've none (says he) I'm going another way,
I'le keep my *conscience*, and the *Church obey*
This said my *witty* Friend with cruel spight,
Leaves me even when the *Butcher*'s going to smite.   [pp. 231-32]

Cowley's affected High-Church scruples about observing fast days must have seemed as outlandish in the London of Charles II as Horace's having Fuscus worry about a possibly fictitious Jewish holy day. But though Sprat was clever in finding equivalents for Horace's speakers, his attempts at a Horatian style were as unuccessful as Brome's. His padded couplets are colloquial, but have none of the force of the compressed Latin original.

There is even more local color in Sprat's portion of the sixth satire of the second book. Notice what happens when the busybody importunes Horace for the latest political gossip, a passage that overlaps and continues the one quoted from Fanshawe in the last chapter.

> . . . "o bone—nam te
> scire, deos quoniam propius contingis, oportet—,
> numquid de Dacis audisti?" "nil equidem." "ut tu
> semper eris derisor." "at omnes di exagitent me,
> si quicquam." "quid militibus promissa Triquetra

praeda Caesar an est Itala tellure daturus?"
iurantem me scire nihil mirantur ut unum
scilicet egregii mortalem altique silenti.   [51-58]

["My dear fellow—you ought to know because you're in close touch
with the top people—have you heard anything about the Dacians?"
"Nothing indeed." "You're always such a joker." "May all the gods
confound me if I ever heard anything." "Well then, is Caesar going to
give allotments of Italian or Sicilian land to the soldiers?" As I swear I
know nothing they marvel and think me a model of discretion.]

Sprat's inquisitive nuisances are also eager for the latest news, but
this time it is of current events of interest to contemporary
Englishmen.

Y'are well met Sir, you know without dispute
How matters goe; (say they) *for now your are*
Acquainted with all States-men secrets here.
And how? and how? and when d'ye expect the Fleet?
When will the King set forth the Queen to meet?
I know not. *Come you'r such another man!*
Let all the *Gods* their judgments on me rain,
If I know any thing. *And what d'ye hear,*
When did the Portuguez *resign* Tangier?
Is all in Ireland *quiet still or no?*
When will my Lord Lieutenant *thither goe?*
Which way are things accommodated there?
For the old Irish, *or the Purchaser?*
Still I persist that I do nothing know,
At my reserv'dness they much wonder shew;
That I'm a close and trusty man they swear,
Fit to be made a *Privy-counsellor.*   [pp. 284-85]

Tangier had been a Portuguese possession and was given to Great
Britain in 1662 as part of the dowry of Catherine of Braganza. It
was as hot an item as Horace's Dacians. So too was whether the
"old Irish" (that is, Gaelic-speaking Roman Catholics) or the new
class of English landlords—many selected from Cromwell's ser-
geants—would be favored in Ireland. Surely Sprat would never

have introduced such striking anachronisms merely "to make the Roman poet more open to English readers." Only a reader who read Latin could enjoy spotting the parallels, which is the essential pleasure an Imitation offers. Sprat's actual audience was the learned reader, someone like Cowley himself, whose version of the rest of the poem foreshadows Pope's blend of the conversational and the heroic.

Although Cowley's *Davideis* is hardly read today even by seventeenth-century specialists, it is the first English epic to display neoclassical elegance in heroic-couplet poetry—Dryden parodies it in *MacFlecknoe*. So when Horace's city mouse speaks in the *sermo urbanus* of a fashionable mouse-about-Rome,

"vis tu homines urbemque feris praeponere silvis?
carpe viam, mihi crede, comes, terrestria quando
mortalis animas vivunt sortita, neque ulla est
aut magno aut parvo leti fuga: quo, bone, circa,
dum licet, in rebus iucundis vive beatus,
vive memor, quam sis aevi brevis. . . ."   [2.6.92-97]

["Wouldn't you prefer men and cities to the wild woods? Take the way. Trust me, chum, earthly creatures have mortal souls; nor is there any escape from death for any creature great or small. While we may, my dear, let's live happily surrounded by pleasant things, mindful of the brevity of life. . . ."]

Cowley's city mouse speaks as a minor character from a Restoration comedy, promising to introduce his country bumpkin cousin to the joys of amorous intrigue.

Let Savage Beasts lodge in a Countrey Den,
You should see *Towns*, and *manners*, and know men,
And taste the *generous* luxury of the Court
Where all the Mice of qualitie resort,
Where thousand beauteous *shees* about you move,
And by high fare are *pliant* made to *love*.
"We all ere long must render up our breath
"No Cave or Hole can shelter us from Death;
"Since life is so uncertain and so short
"Let's spend it all in feasting and in sport."   [pp. 287-88]

When the mice arrive at the house of the rich man, Horace gives the time of night in an elevated epic paraphrasis: "iamque tenebat / nox medium caeli spatium . . ." (Now night held the middle space of heaven, 100-1). Here Cowley the epic poet steps in with two mock-heroic couplets worthy of Alexander Pope's parodic manual on how to write bad verse, *Peri Bathous.*

It was the time when witty Poets tell,
That Phoebus *into* Tethys *Bosome fell,*
She blusht at first, and then put out her light
And drew the modest Curtains *of the night.*

But although Cowley is by far the better poet, in some ways he is more literal than Sprat. He even follows Horace in having the mice's dinner interrupted by watchdogs, not, as we should expect in England, by cats. Yet Cowley extended Fanshawe's discovery that the style of the Horatian *sermo* is often best rendered into heroic couplets almost as smooth, balanced, and elegant, as serious epic requires. Had he lived longer, he might be known as the first of the Augustan satirists, rather than as a belated imitator of Donne whose odes and elegies ran the metaphysical style straight into the ground.

[II]

Unfortunately, it seems to have been the Cowley of the odes who inspired *The Wish, Being the Tenth Satyr of Juvenal Peraphrastically Rendered in Pindarick Verse* (Dublin, 1675), by "a Person, sometimes Fellow of Trin. Col. Dublin." The dedication is signed Edward Wetenhall, and although Wetenhall says the poem was written by a friend, it is hard to believe that anyone but a parent could introduce this brainchild to the world. Most likely Wetenhall was being modest—quite properly—about his literary pretentions. The poem is composed of fifty-six irregular "pindaric" stanzas, the shortest of eight lines, which paraphrase Juvenal very freely. The section in which Juvenal warns that a handsome son brings grief to his parents exhibits Wetenhall's usual standard.

                                          filius autem
corporis egregii miseros trepediosque parentes
semper habet: rara est adeo concordia formae
atque pudicitiae. sanctos licet horrida mores
tradiderit domus ac veteres imitata Sabinos,
praeterea castum ingenium voltumque modesto
sanguine ferventem tribuat natura benigna
larga manu (quid enim puero conferre potest plus
custode aut cura natura potentior omni?):
non licet esse viros. nam prodiga corruptoris
improbitas ipsos audet temptare parentes:
tanta in muneribus fiducia. nullus ephebum
deformem saeva castravit in arce tyrannus,
nec praetextatum rapuit Nero loripedem nec
strumosum atque utero pariter gibboque tumentem.
I nunc et iuvenis specie laetare tui, quem
maiora expectant discrimina . . .   [295–311]

[A son with a handsome body, however, always has wretched and fearful
parents. Rarely do good looks and modesty coincide. Though an austere
home that imitates the ancient Sabines has given him pure morals, and
kind nature also has bestowed with a lavish hand a chaste mind and a
countenance rosy with modest blood (what more indeed can nature,
whose care is better than any guardian's, give?): they are not permitted
to become men. For the immense wickedness of a corruptor dares tempt
the parents themselves; such is the power of gifts. No tyrant ever
castrated a deformed youth in his savage castle. Nero never ravished a
boy with a clubfoot or with the mange, or a hunchback. Go now and
delight in the good looks of your boy, whom greater dangers await.]

Not surprisingly, Wetenhall does not expatiate on the dangers of
castration—a fate that in his time only befell Italian boys with
good voices. Instead he substituted for Juvenal's sensational effects
some very strange conceits of his own.

    A Son, too, if exceeding fair,
    Costs his parents double care,
  In others love, in them he begets fear,
  One chast and handsome we so seldom find,

You'd think such bodies ne're did suit the mind.
 Though the House whence he took his blood
 Be course and plain as the old *Sabines* were,
  And gave him documents as severe
  Nay though his disposition's good,
  Though Nature has done all she can,
  (Honest Nature far exceeding
  All the tricks and cheats of breeding.)
 Though she bestows on him a modest look,
 The happy *Index* of a well writ Book,
And with a Mint of blood his face has lin'd,
  Ready in blushes to be coin'd;
  When she has giv'n him all this store,
 And she, though liberal, can give no more:
  After all this, O Beauty's curse!
  He shall Eunuch be or worse,
The World will never suff'r him to live good, or man. [p. 27]

I cannot think of a form less like the dactylic hexameter, with its heavy measured cadences, than the irregular ode. Juvenal drives us forward as he piles on hyperbole after hyperbole. Wetenhall treats us to a series of pious ejaculations and holds our attention only because we have no idea what is to come next. Perhaps Wetenhall thought that the elevated style and morality of the tenth satire required the stylistic and metrical extravagance of the greater ode, and like Swift twenty years later, attempted to soar beyond his powers. At least Wetenhall, unlike some other translators, fairly estimated his abilities, and abandoned the muse for whatever drudge in the celestial recording office inspires theological and ecclesiastical prose, and finished his career as a bishop in the Church of Ireland, an achievement that was to elude a much more talented satirist in the next century.

[III]

Although Sprat and Cowley wrote the earliest Imitations of Horace, John Wilmot, Earl of Rochester, first used the Imitation as a weapon to attack contemporaries. His "Allusion to Horace" (probably written in 1675), like its inspiration the tenth satire of the first book, is directed against literary bad taste. The Imitation, however, is openly much more aggressive than its model, and Rochester's target—unlike Horace's—is a living poet, John Dryden. The origin of the quarrel between Rochester and Dryden is obscure. They led rival literary coteries, and Rochester had already satirized Dryden's patron, the Earl of Mulgrave. Probably simple jealousy and the hauteur of an aristocratic amateur toward a mercenary professional gave Rochester impetus enough to take on Dryden. But the opening of his Imitation is strange, and suggests that Rochester had written against Dryden previously, although such a critique is unknown to scholarship. For as Rochester's modern editor notes, "An Allusion to Horace" is the earliest overt sign of the enmity between Rochester and Dryden."[6] Yet Rochester begins

Well, sir, 'tis granted I said Dryden's rhymes
Were stol'n, unequal, nay dull many times.
What foolish patron is there found of his
So blindly partial to deny me this?
But that his plays, embroidered up and down
With wit and learning, justly pleased the town
In the same paper I as freely own.

Both "I said" and "in the same paper" certainly imply that Rochester had satirized Dryden earlier, and in writing, not just in conversation.[7] The "Allusion" is not at all Horatian, if we accept the conventional notion that Horatian satire is gentle and smiling, but then neither is Horace's original, at least for the "turgid Alp man" (36) and Demetrius and Tigellius (90). But when Rochester forgets about Dryden, he can be quite delightfully "Horatian," as in his version of Horace's advice on how to achieve a correct satiric style. Horace advised:

ergo non satis est risu diducere rictum
auditoris; et est quaedam tamen hic quoque virtus.
est brevitate opus, ut currat sententia neu se

impediat verbis lassas onerantibus auris,
et sermone opus est modo tristi, saepe iocoso,
defendente vicem modo rhetoris atque poetae,
interdum urbani, parcentis viribus atque
extenuantis eas consulto. ridiculum acri
fortius et melius magnas plerumque secat res.   [7-15]

[So it is not enough to draw a laugh from a gaping listener, though even
this has some value. The object is conciseness, so that the thoughts flow
and do not clog tired ears with burdensome words. And the diction
should sometimes be serious and sometimes funny, taking in turn the
style of the orator and of the poet, and occasionally of the man of wit,
sparing its strength and pulling its punches. Often ridicule will cut
through knotty problems more ably and better than seriousness.]

So Rochester suggests:

But within due proportions circumscribe
Whate'er you write, that with a flowing tide
The style may rise, yet in its rise forbear
With useless words t'oppress the wearied ear.
Here be your language lofty, there more light:
Your rhetoric with your poetry unite.
For elegance' sake, sometimes allay the force
Of epithets: 'twill soften the discourse.
A jest in scorn points out and hits the thing
More home than the morosest satyr's sting.   [20-29]

Rochester's unbalanced couplets match the original hexameters,
which use such clumsy verse endings as "sententia neu se" and
"plerumque secat res"—Augustan poets generally avoid monosyllables in the last foot. (Too often in comparing a translation with
its original—Pope's Homer is a conspicuous example—we ignore
the translator's handling of effects that do not come through in a
literal translation, as if meter—and often poetic vocabulary—were
not as much a part of the original as the literal sense.)

Unfortunately, Rochester did not follow his own advice to
avoid the "morosest satyr's sting" when dealing with Dryden, and
it is then that Rochester diverges most from Horace. Horace

wisely confined himself to questions of technique and literary
standards, attacking only Lucilius' modern admirers. For Lucilius
himself Horace affects a high opinion, praising him as the inventor
of satire and as Horace's great predecessor. Although Rochester
appeals to literary standards, it is Dryden's lack of social grace and
aristocratic ease that arouses his scorn. After praising the amatory
poetry of Sir Charles Sedley, Rochester continues, with no warrant at all from Horace:

> Dryden in vain tried this nice way of wit,
> For he to be a tearing blade thought fit.
> But when he would be sharp, he still was blunt:
> To frisk his frolic fancy, he'd cry, "Cunt!"
> Would give the ladies a dry bawdy bob,
> And thus he got the name of Poet Squab.   [71-76]

But then Rochester returnes to Horace, who says of Lucilius,
"neque ego detrahere ausim / haerentem capiti cum multa laude
coronam" (nor would I dare deprive him of the crown that clings
to his head with much praise, 48-49), a sentiment uniquely apt
when the subject is quite literally poet laureate.

> But, to be just, 'twill to his praise be found
> His excellencies more than faults abound;
> Nor dare I from his sacred temples tear
> That laurel which he best deserves to wear.   [77-80]

Of course Rochester may have been implying, like Pope in the
case of George II and Colley Cibber, that Charles II had the
laureate he deserved.

Rochester's pose of Horatian moderation deceived no one, least
of all Dryden himself.[8] The "Allusion" strains our credulity in
trying to picture Dryden as Lucilius. Dryden was not a rough and
ready amateur (a description that better fits Rochester himself)
who accidently created a new literary genre for his successors to
perfect, but a hard-working professional trying to bring contemporary literature to a high standard of critical excellence, a writer

who resembled Lucilius not at all, but Horace very much.[9] The problem is not that the "Allusion" is "unfair"—so is *MacFlecknoe*. The problem is that the reader who keeps Horace in mind, as the reader of an Imitation should, cannot help being constantly reminded of how poorly Dryden fits the paradigm of battered old relic of obsolete literary taste. It is as if, say, one were attacking contemporary American novelists for slavish devotion to nineteenth-century conventions of realism and using as the prime offender Thomas Pynchon. The "Allusion" really needed a Dryden who modeled his style on Spenser's.

[IV]

The most effective answer to Rochester's "Allusion" as not Dryden's "Preface" to *All for Love*, but another Horatian Imitation, Sir Carr Scroope's "In Defense of Satire" (1677), loosely based on the fourth satire of the first book. Apparently Scroope had been provoked by his portrait in the "Allusion":

Should I be troubl'd when the purblind knight,
Who squints more in his judgment than his sight,
Picks silly faults and censures what I write.   [115-17]

In spite of his unprepossessing appearance, Scroope had some pretentions to being a lover and a love poet, pretentions Rochester satirized brilliantly in his deliciously obscene "Mock Song." But as a satirist and as an imitator of Horace, Scroope was not out of his league in challenging Rochester.

Horace began by tracing satire (inaccurately but effectively) back to Athenian Old Comedy.

Eupolis atque Cratinus Aristophanesque poetae
atque alii, quorum comoedia prisca virorum est,
siquis erat dignus describi, quod malus ac fur,
quod moechus foret aut sicarius aut alioqui
famosus, multa cum libertate notabant.

[The poets Eupolis and Cratinus and Aristophanes and others, who invented Old Comedy, pointed out whoever deserved to be satirized, whether he was evil, a thief, an adulterer, a murderer, or otherwise infamous, with great freedom of speech.]

According to Horace, Lucilius adopted their methods but changed their meters ("hinc omnis pendet Lucilius, hosce secutus, / mutatis tantum pedibus numerisque . . ."), unfortunately in a style that was careless and uncouth. Scroope's Imitation begins with an English counterpart for Old Comedy, but then takes another direction.

When Shakespeare, Jonson, Fletcher rul'd the stage,
They took so bold a freedom with the age
That there was scarce a knave or fool in town
Of any note but had his picture shown.
And without doubt, though some it may offend,
Nothing helps more than satire to amend
Ill manners, or is trulier virtue's friend.
Princes may laws ordain, priest gravely preach,
But poets most successfully will teach.[10]

Instead of finding an equivalent for Lucilius, Scroope ignored his original to create a portrait of the satirist as a public benefactor upholding moral standards. It was to remain one of the standard defenses of the satirist.[11] Perhaps Scroope remembered the first satire of the second book, where Horace placed Lucilius in that role (62-70), and decided to describe it here. Of course Scroope's real purpose in defending satire and the satirist—as it would be for Pope—was to camouflage satiric attacks against specific individuals. Usually Scroope disguises his targets under pseudo-classical or theatrical names, such as Simius, Cully, Alidore, Bessus, and Cornus; but from manuscript glosses it appears that contemporaries knew their real identities. Not that it matters most of the time to us. The vices satirized are so common and the sinners now so obscure that knowing whom the pseudonyms conceal scarcely matters. But in one case the context is very important. Horace had his imaginary interlocutor say that the satirist enjoys hurting

people: " 'Laedere gaudes,' inquis, / 'et hoc studio pravus facis' "
("You love to hurt people," you say, "you're a knave and do it
intentionally," 78-79). As usual, this interlocutor sets up a reply
by the satirist, giving Horace a chance to expatiate on who the real
knaves are.

> . . . unde petitum
> hoc in me iacis? est auctor quis denique eorum,
> vixi cum quibus? absentem qui rodit, amicum
> qui non defendit alio culpante, solutos
> qui captat risus hominum famamque dicacis,
> fingere qui non visa potest, conmissa tacere
> qui nequit: hic niger est, hunc tu, Romane, caveto. [79-85]

[Where do you get this accusation you throw at me? Is the inventor
anyone of those with whom I've lived? The man who slanders someone
behind his back, who does not defend his friend when someone blames
him, who wants to get belly laughs and to be known as a wit, who makes
up things he's never seen, and who is unable to keep a secret, this is the
one black of heart, him, O Roman, you should fear.]

Here Scroope found his chance for revenge. Rochester had a
reputation as a wit, probably made things up, and certainly could
not keep a secret—accidently showing Charles II a lampoon he
had written on His Majesty was perhaps Rochester's most amusing indiscretion. Much better yet, Rochester had been involved
in a particularly disgraceful brawl, at Epsom, 17 June 1676, and
apparently behaved as a coward. Rochester deserted a friend
named Downs, who had kept him from assaulting a constable,
leaving Downs to be killed by the watch, who thought him the
assailant.[12] In such a context Horace's "amicum qui non defendit"
acquired a new application.

> He that can rail at one he calls his friend,
> Or hear him absent wrong'd, and not defend,
> Who for the sake of some ill-natur'd jest
> Tells what he should conceal, invents the rest,
> To fatal midnight frolics can betray

His brave companion and then run away,
Leaving him to be murder'd in the street,
Then put it off with some buffoon conceit,
This, this is he you should beware of all,
Yet him a witty, pleasant man you call.
To whet your dull debauches up and down,
You seek him as top fiddler of the town.   [48-59]

The "buffoon conceit" may be Rochester's poem, "To the Post-boy," in which Rochester, confesses among other offenses

Frighted at my own mischiefs, I have fled
And bravely left my life's defender dead;
Broke houses to break chastity, and dyed
That floor with murder which my lust denied.

And then he asks, "the readiest way to Hell," to which the postboy responds, "The readiest way, my Lord, 's Rochester." In the best satiric portraits, such as Dryden's of Zimri in *Absalom and Achitophel*, the target's virtues are turned deftly into vices, as here Rochester's wit and ability to satirize himself become a "buffoon conceit." Of course the "fatal midnight frol-ics" owe nothing to Horace, but Scroope has inserted them so neatly that they blend in with details adapted from the original. Unlike Rochester's substitution of Dryden for Lucilius, where we cannot help but notice the violence of the switch from a rustic amateur to a slick professional, here it seems quite appropriate that the backbiter and scoffer should turn out also to be a knave and a coward. And by not naming Rochester directly, Scroope avoids the appearance of malicious libel without the shadowboxing of general satire that characterizes so much of the rest of the poem. By referring to an incident whose perpetrator was unmistakable, Scroope could abuse Rochester while maintaining the pose of disinterested moralist. "In Defense of Satire" is not a particularly witty or amusing poem, but its author should receive credit as the first to booby-trap an apparently innocuous original by adding a few, seemingly harmless, details. The bomb must have exploded, for in "On the Supposed Author of a Late Poem in Defense of Satire" Rochester forgot all about the pose of Horatian moderation and fell back into the "railing" style of "satyr," labeling Scroope an "ass" and "an ugly *beau garcon*, / Spit at and shunned by every girl in town." Scroope shrugged off Rochester's insults with a six-line epigram beginning, "Rail on, poor scribbler, speak of me / In as bad terms as the world speaks of thee," confident of having had the best of the exchange.

The Imitation Is Perfected

One satirist who seems to have remained on decent terms with both Rochester and Dryden was John Oldham. Unfortunately, his critical reputation today comes from Dryden's famous elegy, "To the Memory of Mr. Oldham," in which Dryden asks rhetorically:

O early ripe! to thy abundant store
What could advancing Age have added more?
It might (what Nature never gives the young)
Have taught the numbers of thy native Tongue.
But Satyr needs not those, and Wit will shine
Through the harsh cadence of a rugged line.
A noble Error, and but seldom made,
When Poets are by too much force betray'd.   [11–18]

This picture of Oldham's poetry as the work of a satirical back-alley fighter partly fits his *Satires upon the Jesuits* (1681), but not at all Oldham's Imitations of Horace's ninth satire of the first book and the third and thirteenth satires of Juvenal. Oldham was a kind of literary chameleon, who adapted whatever style seemed appropriate to his speaker. When it is a libertine like Rochester, in the "Satyr against Vertue," or Father Garnett, in the *First Satire upon the Jesuits*, Oldham teeters on the edge of bathos as he tries to make these monsters of depravity rant in an appropriate style. But the more restrained and understated style of Horace brought out Oldham's best. As James Sutherland put it: "His rendering of the ninth Satire of the first Book ('As I was walking in the Mall of late') is a little masterpiece, beautifully lively and colloquial; a Restoration poem that happened to be written by a Latin poet sixteen hundred years earlier."[1] Oldham calls the impertinent bore who interrupts his solitary walk, "a familiar Fop" and a "Cox-comb." The bore turns out to be even more garrulous than Horace's, and Oldham is more circumstantial in telling us what he had to say. Horace's "cum quidlibet ille / garriret, vicos, urbem laudaret" (yet he babbled on as he pleased, praising the neighbor-hood and the city, 12-13) becomes Oldham's[2]

He all the while baits me with tedious chat,
Speaks much about the drought, and how the rate
Of Hay is raised, and what it now goes at:
Tells me of a new Comet at the *Hague*,
Portending God knows what, a Dearth, or Plague:
Names every Wench, that passes through the Park,
How much she is allow'd, and who the Spark,
That keeps her: points, who lately got a Clap,
And who at the *Groom-porters* had ill hap
Three nights ago, in play with such a Lord.
[pp. 46-47 (misnumbered for 45-46)]

But in the summer of 1681 there was a much more pressing question than the price of hay (no trivial matter, though—hay was then what oil is for us),[3] namely the Popish Plot and the resulting Exclusion Crisis.

Next he begins to plague me with the *Plot*,
Asks, whether I were known to *Oats* or not?
"Not I, 'thank Heaven! I no Priest have been:
"Have never Doway, *nor* St. Omers *seen,*
What think you, Sir; will they Fitz-Harris *try?*
Will he die, think you? Yes, most certainly.
I mean, be hang'd. "Would thou wert so (wish'd I.)   [pp. 48-49]

Oldham's bore is not merely tactless, but dangerous as well as he suggests that Oldham might be on Titus Oates's list of Popish conspirators. (Breaking the long-moribund rule of not identifying an author with his "persona" makes the bore even more insulting and ill-informed. Imagine asking the author of *Satires upon the Jesuits* if he belonged to the society.) Douai was the continental headquarters of the English Roman Catholics and St. Omer a Jesuit seminary Oates had attended (and from which he had been expelled, apparently for buggery). After Oldham has denied vehemently that he had anything to do with the Papists, the bore cannot leave the dangerous topic alone and wants to know what Oldham thinks the fate will be of Edward Fitzharris, a Roman Catholic accused, falsely, of plotting to murder the king. He was indeed hanged, on 1 July 1681. In later editions Oldham had the bore change tacks and enquire about the other side, asking, *"What think you, Sir: Will they the* Joyner *try?"* He was referring to Stephen College, known as the "Protestant Joiner," because of the former carpenter's ceaseless clamor against Roman Catholic plots, which, of course, College found everywhere. He was also hanged, 31 August 1681, for "a most scandalous libel against the government" called *A Raree Show*.[4] Horace, of course, would never have risked the bore's bringing up anything that might prove politically embarrassing. But characteristically Horatian is Oldham's weaving everyday conversation into verse (cf. the talk between Maecenas and Horace in *Satires* 2.6.44-45). The bore's attempt to wiggle his way into the good graces of Oldham's patron (identified only as "His Grace") does not come off so well. Oldham's patron remains a shadowy figure, as good taste doubtless dictated he should. (He was, in fact, the Earl of Kingston.) This reserve is typical among Horace's Imitators, even Pope, perhaps because it is hard to be candid, which demands spontaneity, while pretending to another poet's personality.

At the end of the poem, when Horace finally despairs ever escaping, the bore is suddenly seized and dragged into court to serve as a witness. Oldham's relief is equally unexpected, and even less pleasant for the bore.

> While I was thus lamenting my ill hap,
> Comes aid at length: a brace of Bailiffs clap

> The Rascal on the back: *"Here take your Fees,*
> *"Kind Gentlemen* (said I) *for my release.*
> He would have had me Bail. *"Excuse me, Sir,*
> *"I've made a Vow ne'er to be Surety more:*
> *"My Father was undone by't heretofore.*
> 　Thus I got off, and bless'd the Fates that he
> 　Was Pris'ner made, I set at liberty.　　　　　[pp. 52-53]

Although Oldham is not quite so playful as Horace, he catches the style of the Horatian *sermo pedestris* very nicely. If the Imitation of *Satires* 1.9 were better known, Dryden's description of Oldham in the elegy would be received with appropriate skepticism (Dryden was, of course, trying to set up Oldham as his John the Baptist of satire).

[II]

Surprisingly, the received opinion of Oldham's style is not based on his Imitations of Juvenal, which are even more neglected than the *Satires upon the Jesuits*. The Imitation of the third satire has sometimes been read by Johnsonians ever since Boswell discovered that Oldham had anticipated Johnson's *London* in turning the despised Greeks into Frenchmen. But the Imitation of the thirteenth satire shares the modern unpopularity of its now neglected original, which once ranked with the tenth satire as a moral treatise and arsenal of virtuous *sententiae* and which provided the epigraph for Johnson's *Rambler* No. 185 on the folly of desiring revenge.

　　Oldham shows himself alert to extract new effects from the original, noticing a word here and there and giving it a completely new context. In the thirteenth satire, Juvenal tells his friend Calvinus, defrauded by an untrustworthy friend, that with the crime rate skyrocketing as it is these days, losing a mere ten thousand sesterces is hardly worth noticing.

magna quidem, sacris quae dat praecepta libellis,
victrix fortunae sapientia; ducimus autem

hos quoque felices, qui ferre incommoda vitae
nec iactare iugum vita didicere magistra.
quae tam festa dies, ut cesset prodere furem,
perfidiam, fraudes atque omni ex crimine lucrum
quaesitum et partos gladio vel pyxide nummos?
rari quippe boni: numera, vix sunt totidem quot
Thebarum portae vel divitis ostia Nili.
nona aetas agitur peioraque saecula ferri
temporibus, quorum sceleri non invenit ipsa
nomen et a nullo posuit natura metallo.
nos hominum divumque fidem clamore ciemus,
quanto Faesidium laudat vocalis agentem
sportula? . . .   [19–33]

[Philosophy, however, who delivers her precepts in sacred books is great
indeed and knows how to overcome fortune; we regard those also as
happy who with life as a teacher have learned to bear life's misfortunes
instead of casting off the yoke. What day, however festal, is there that
fails to bring to light a thief, deceit, fraud, and money sought through
every kind of crime, either with the sword or with poison. Good men
are few. Count them. They are scarcely as numerous as the gates of
Thebes or the mouths of the Nile. The Ninth Age is passing, an age
worse than the Iron Age, for whose crime nature herself cannot find a
name derived from a base enough metal. We summon the faith of men
and gods as loudly as the noisy dole (that is, his clients) praises Faesidius
when he is pleading a case.]

Oldham's version is longer by eight lines, which is not too much,
considering the greater terseness of the Latin, for an elevated
passage full of mock-epic paraphrases and clever allusions.

    Almighty Wisdom gives in Holy Writ
Wholsome Advice to all, that follow it:
And those, that will not its great Counsels hear,
May learn from meer experience how to bear
(Without vain strugling) Fortune's yoke, and how
They ought her rudest shocks to undergo.
There's not a day so solemn through the year,
Not one red Letter in the Calendar,

> But we of some new Crime discover'd hear.
> Theft, Murder, Treason, Perjury, what not?
> Moneys by Cheating, Padding, Poisoning got.
> Nor is it strange; so few are now the Good,
> That fewer scarce were left at *Noah*'s Flood:
> Should *Sodom*'s Angel here in Fire descend,
> Our Nation wants ten Men to save the Land.
> Fate has reserv'd us for the very Lees
> Of time, where Ill admits of no degrees:
> An Age so bad old Poets ne'r could frame,
> Nor find a Metal out to give't a name.
> This your experience knows; and yet for all
> On faith of God, and Man aloud you call,
> Louder than on Queen *Bess*'s day the Rout
> For *Antichrist* burnt in Effigie shout.   [pp. 27-28]

The couplet technique is not much better than Rochester's or Scroope's, with excessive enjambments, weak rhymes ("how" / "undergo," "not" / "got"), and otiose adjectives to help out the meter. But Juvenal's tone (which is not simply the railing invective handbooks call "Juvenalian") comes through clearly as Oldham combines admonitions that point out the obvious with outrageous hyperboles expressing the total depravity of society. Oldham's counterparts for Juvenal's details are even nicer, both surprising and apt: the Bible for Stoic philosophy (virtually a religion in Juvenal's time anyway), the liturgical year for the *fasti*, the events narrated in the seventh and ninth chapters of Genesis (did Oldham forget that two angels were sent to Sodom?) for the traditional seven gates of Thebes and seven mouths of the Nile, and allusions to the Popish Plot to add to Juvenal's calendar of contemporary crimes—"murder, treason, perjury, what not?"— with a Pope-burning pageant that must have been much louder than Faesidius' claque of clients at their most vociferous. Only the Hesiodic Iron Age escaped Oldham's efforts to find a contemporary equivalent and forced him to be content with translating the original.

Oldham's version of the third satire deserves to be read for its own sake, and not as an uncouth precursor of Johnson's *London;*

despite their common ancestor the two poems are quite different, and comparison is not really fair to either. Although Oldham made allusions to contemporary events, his Imitation is not a political satire like *London*. It is also much longer, develops more slowly, but parallels Juvenal more closely than *London*, and refers much more frequently to specific persons. Some are real, such as Morecraft the head-dresser, Gadbury the almanac-maker, Pordage the poetaster, and the mysterious aeronaught Johnston.⁵ Others are taken from literature—Sir Sidrophel and Sir Martin Marr-all. As in the Imitation of Horace, *Satires* 1.9, the best touches in Oldham's version of Juvenal's third satire are the vivid details of daily life in a huge metropolis divided between a tiny wealthy elite—an elite that includes a good many parvenu vulgarians—and an impoverished mass of ordinary citizens who cannot afford the minimum requisite for a safe and healthy life. We experience what it feels like to be trapped in the top story of a burning house, trampled by jostling crowds of disgusting foreigners, and threatened with street accidents by day and footpads and assailants by night. Here Oldham is worlds better than Johnson. Oldham's fidelity to the structure of the original, even at the cost of writing a much longer poem, gives a chance to create English examples almost as memorable as Juvenal's, such as the portrait of the poor poet who lost everything he had in a fire.

lectus erat Codro Procula minor, urceoli sex
ornamentum abaci nec non et parvulus infra
cantharus et recubans sub eodem marmore Chiron;
iamque vetus Graecos servabat cista libellos
et divina opici rodebant carmina mures.
nil habuit Codrus, quis enim negat? et tamen illud
perdidit infelix totum nihil. ultimus autem
aerumnae cumulus, quod nudum et frustra rogantem
nemo cibo, nemo hospitio tectoque iuvabit.   [203-11]

[Codrus had a bed too small for Procula, six pitchers adorning his sideboard and also a tin tankard underneath, and a reclining Chiron under the same marble (sideboard). And an old bookcase held little

Greek books and barbarous mice gnawed the divine poems. Codrus had nothing, who denies it? And yet the poor wretch lost even that nothing. The worst burden of poverty is that no one will help him, naked and begging in vain, with a meal or with a hospitable roof.]

Before we notice that Oldham seems unfeeling and hardhearted in his attitude towards the poor poet,[6] we should remember that in the seventeenth and eighteenth centuries the Codrus who suffered the fire was thought to be the same as the "hoarse Codrus," the poetaster who perpetrated the terrible *Theseid* mentioned by Juvenal at the beginning of the first satire, and thus a byword for poetic incompetence. (Modern texts usually give that name as "Cordus," following the best manuscript.) So in the second book of the *Dunciad* Pope has Dulness give Curll "A shaggy Tap'stry, worthy to be spread / On Codrus' old, or Dunton's modern bed" (143-44). For a contemporary denizen of Grub Street, Oldham turned to Samuel Pordage, a poet so obscure we cannot even be sure what he wrote.[7] (He may have been the author of two Whig attempts to answer Dryden's *Absalom and Achitophel* and *The Medal*, entitled *Azaria and Hushai* and *The Medal Revers'd*.)

> The moveables of *P[orda]ge* were a Bed
> For him, and's Wife, a Piss-pot by its side,
> A Looking-glass upon the Cupboards Head,
> A Comb-case, Candlestick, and Pewter-spoon,
> For want of Plate, with a Desk to write upon:
> A Box without a Lid serv'd to contain
> Few Authors, which made up his *Vatican:*
> And there his own immortal Works were laid,
> On which the barbarous Mice for hunger prey'd;
> *P[ordage]* had nothing, all the World does know;
> And yet should he have lost this Nothing too,
> No one the wretched Bard would have suppli'd
> With Lodging, House-room, or a Crust of Bread.   [p. 197]

Pordage's wife is here because seventeenth-century commentators thought Procula was Codrus' wife (modern scholars think

Procula was a dwarf). The domestic details are good; Pordage seems to be even more penurious than Codrus (though marble was very cheap in ancient Rome). Oldham keeps the "barbarous mice" of Juvenal, though his point seems to get lost, since "opici" means not just "uncivilized," but specifically "ignorant of Greek." Oldham's barbarous mice are actually showing excellent taste, since they are devouring Pordage's "immortal Works"—an ironic oxymoron worthy of the narrator of *Tale of a Tub*, as is calling Pordage's minuscule collection of books a Vatican library. One trouble, unfortunately, with using real examples is that the Imitator must stick to the facts. Apparently Pordage was never victim of a fire, so Oldham has to put Pordage's loss into the subjunctive—"yet should he have lost"—which is hardly as affecting as the plight of Codrus, who really lost ("perdidit") everything. But if we assume that Juvenal's original audience were supposed to know who Codrus was, Oldham's substitution of an actual person seems appropriate.

In the encounter with the drunken bully—one of the terrors of the night—Oldham's "Scowrer" (as such thugs were called in Oldham's time; in the early eighteenth century they were called "Mohocks" or "Hectors") gives away little in insolence and sadistic glee to Juvenal's "ebrius et petulans, qui nullum forte cecidit" (a drunken bravo who perchance hasn't killed anybody yet) who stops the poor man on his way home and fires a barrage of insulting questions at him.

. . . "unde venis?" exclamat "cuius aceto,
cuius conche tumes? quis tecum sectile porrum
sutor et elixi vervecis labra comedit?
nil mihi respondes? aut dic aut accipe calcem.
ede ubi consistas, in qua te quaero proseucha?"   [292-96]

["Where do you come from?" he shouts. "Whose cheap plonk and beans are you full of? What shoemaker ate sliced leek and boiled sheep's lips with you? You won't answer me? Speak up or get kicked. Where's your stand? In what synagogue will I find you?"]

Oldham's scowrer is even more scornful about the poor man's probable way of earning his living.

Who's there? he cries, and takes you by the Throat,
Dog! are you dumb? Speak quickly, else my Foot
Shall march about your Buttocks: whence d'ye come,
From what Bulk-ridden Strumpet reeking home?
Saving you reverend Pimpship, where d'ye ply?
How may one have a Job of Lechery?   [p. 203]

"We note the tang of real speech."[8] Take away the unobtrusive rhymes and it sounds like something Lord Rochester or one of his friends said to the unfortunate barber who found them tossing fiddlers in a blanket the night of that fatal brawl at Epsom. There are no realistic touches like these in Johnson's *London*. Curiously, we find Oldham sounding most like Juvenal when Juvenal sounded— if we ignore the violence of the episode—most like Horace, adapting everyday life and conversation to verse that does not pretend to be serious poetry. But however inferior Oldham the stylist was to Juvenal, he was up to the mark set by his master as a social satirist. When the long-awaited Clarendon Press edition of Oldham finally appears, which will explain the multitude of details and allusions to contemporary life, Oldham's Imitation should be as interesting for its picture of social life in Restoration London as the third satire is for Imperial Rome.[9] There is a lot of Juvenal in Oldham, but it is not the Juvenal that the student of artistic technique is likely to notice. Where the pedestrian muse takes over from Melpomene, and she often does in the third and thirteenth satires, Oldham can stand comparison with his Roman original as well as any Imitator besides Alexander Pope at his best. When the Imitations start receiving critical attention in their own right, instead of being treated as crude attempts to emulate Samuel Johnson (much as the *Satires upon the Jesuits* are contrasted with the satires of Dryden), Oldham's reputation should change very much for the better.

[III]

Although Oldham is undervalued for want of decent modern texts, he is a household name compared to Thomas Wood, whose

Juvenalis Redivivus, or the First Satyr of Juvenal Taught to Speak Plain English (1683) has never been reprinted, much less edited. But though a very minor poet, Wood was a major innovator in the development of the Imitation, whose work deserves to be much better known. So far as I have been able to discover, he is the first Imitator to combine literary and political satire. The first satire of Juvenal is an ideal vehicle for both, as it begins with a contrast between the vapid artificiality of contemporary poetry, particularly epic, and the current luxuriance of social decay and moral corruption. Every satirist knows that he lives in a time of debased literary and moral standards, so it is odd that the first satire has not been more popular with Imitators, though allusions and quotations turn up everywhere.

Juvenal began the first satire by deploring the presence of bad poets everywhere.

Semper ego auditor tantum? numquamne reponam,
vexatus totiens rauci Theseide Codri?
inpune ergo mihi recitaverit ille togatas,
hic elegos? inpune diem consumpserit ingens
Telephus aut summi plena iam margine libri
scriptus et in tergo necdum finitus Orestes?
nota magis nulli domus est sua, quam mihi lucus
Martis et Aeoliis vicinum rupibus antrum
Vulcani; quid agant venti, quas torqueat umbras
Aeacus, unde alius furtivae devehat aurum
pelliculae, quantas iaculetur Monychus ornos,
Frontonis platani convulsaque marmora clamant
semper et adsiduo ruptae lectore columnae.

[Am I always only a listener? Shall I never reply, driven mad by the *Theseid* of hoarse Codrus? Shall that one recite his farces, this one his elegies, to me and escape unpunished? Shall monstrous *Telephus* use up the whole day unpunished, or *Orestes*, written to the edge of the page and on the back and still not finished? Nobody knows his own home as well as I know the grove of Mars and the cave of Vulcan next to the Aeolian rocks; what the winds do, what shades Aeacus tortures, from where another character bore away the gold of the little stolen fleece, how many mountain ashes Monychus throws about, the plane trees of Fronto and the shattered columns and the broken marble cry out from the constant readings.]

Wood goes not to a poetry recitation but to the theatre to experience contemporary literary taste at its most depraved.

> But must I alway[s] suffer this? Can I
> So tamely still an ears *good nature* trie,
> Exalted Nonsense being plac'd for Pillory?
> Must I in *complaisance* conceal my pain?
> No, I'le turn Fool, and write, and *vex* again.
> Dear *Doeg*, long have I with patience heard
> *Cambyses* roar, and mighty thundrings fear'd.
> The Commick *Mamamouch'* hath teiz'd me too
> And *Sappho* with her wondrous Empty shew,
> A *Torie* faith, yet sha'nt unpunish'd go.
> The *Citty* Wits have often scar'd my Eyes
> With *lamentable, mournful* Elegies,
> But of all plagues *Mack Fleckno* is the worst,
> With Guts and Poverty severely curst:
> Large is his Corps, his mighty works do swell,
> Both *carefully* fill'd up, and stuff'd from Hell:
> *Eternal* Sot, *all o're* a publick Ass,
> Is cypher'd in the *margin* of his Face.
> No tawdry Jilt does Playhouse better know,
> Than I St. *Jameses* Park, or who kist who:
> I know *Morefields*, where cunning Bawds do live;
> Th'*Exchange*, where none but Knaves and Cuckolds thrive.

Fortunately, unlike Juvenal's Codrus and the author of the *Orestes*, the performers in Wood's literary flea circus are fairly easy to indentify. Doeg, we recall from Dryden's contribution to the *Second Part of Absalom and Achitophel*, is Elkanah Settle, author of the sensational horror tragedy *Cambyses*. *Mamamouchi* is the alternative title for Edward Ravenscroft's *The Citizen Turn'd Gentleman*, an immensely popular but intellectually wholly vacuous comedy, and Sappho of "*Torie* faith" must be Aphra Behn. I reckon the elegies of the City wits were the poems lamenting the murder of Sir Edmund Berry Godfrey that appeared in droves during the Popish Plot hysteria. And with MacFlecknoe we are once again on familiar ground.

Wood's favorable references to contemporary figures are more direct, though sometimes confusing, and call for some knowledge of the more salacious varieties of Restoration literature. In the original, Juvenal contrasted satire with sterile mythological themes.

haec ego non credam Venusina digna lucerna?
haec ego non agitem? sed quid magis? Heracleas
aut Diomedeas aut mugitum labyrinthi
et mare percussum puero fabrumque volantem?   [51-54]

[Shouldn't I think these vices deserve the Venusian lamp (that is, the satires of Horace)? Shouldn't I attack them? What would you prefer? Poems about Hercules or Diomedes or the bellowing in the labyrinth and the sea struck by the boy and the flying inventor?]

Wood does not contrast satire with mythology, but with sex comedy and erotic poetry.

Where's *Auldram Rochester*, and *Wicherley*,
You mighty Souls, that in this Cause dare dye?
Let't draw our Pens, and quit *Tarsander*'s Praise,
Fair *Phillis* lovely *Bum*, the charming ways
Of *Country Wife*, renown'd for mizmaze trickes,
Or where their darts our Courtlike *Cupids* fix.
The Worlds on Fire, it does in madness reign,
Quench it with Ink, with Satyr breath a Vein:
Peevish, perverse, & base, it hates a Cure,
And scarce will our true honest minds endure;
It must, it must the kind *Plain-dealers* feel,
That will its *sores*, and foul *diseases* heal.   [p. 9]

The references to William Wycherley's *Country Wife* and *Plain Dealer* are obvious enough. Wood himself annotated *"Tarsander"* rather smirkingly: "Those that have read the *E[arl] of R[ochester's]* Poems will know very well what I mean by *Tarsander*, but (because I pretend somewhat to Modesty) I shall not explain it at present." The allusion is probably to the dialogue between "Tar-sander" and "Swiveanthe" beginning "For standing tarses we kind Nature thank," which was published in the 1680 edition of Rochester, but was probably written by Buckhurst.[10] The first line in the passage is very perplexing and set me to wondering why Rochester apparently should be referred to as an old Scottish ram, till it occurred to me that the line really ought to read: "Where's *Oldham, Rochester,* and *Wicherley?*"[11] Then the Phillis who possessed the lovely bottom is the subject of Oldham's Imitation of Vincent Voiture, "Upon a Lady, Who by overturning of a Coach, had her Coats behind flung up, and what was under shewn to the View of the Company," which ends:

In pity gentle *Phillis* hide
The dazling Beams of your Back-side;
For should they shine unclouded long,
All human kind would be undone.
Not the bright Goddesses on high,
That reign above the starry Sky,
Should they turn up to open view
All their immortal Tails, can shew
An *Arse-h*—— so divine as you.[12]

The metaphor of the satirist as a physician healing disease is a commonplace in the seventeenth-century; much more original is the similitude of the satirist as a fireman putting out a conflagration of vice in a shower of ink—Wood had a true instinct for the bathetic.

In spite of its ineptitude, *Juvenalis Redivivus* is an important document in the history of the Imitation. It is the first to invite comparison directly with the Latin original by printing it at the bottom of the page, and the first, at least of a satire, to show that its author was aware that the Imitation is a distinct genre with its own rules. Wood also anticipated Pope's discovery that the Imitator could create satiric effects not only by paralleling the original directly, but also by turning it on its head. At the end of the first satire, Juvenal had his *adversarius* warn him that if he expresses himself openly, he will be denounced by an informer, and that he had better stick to safer topics. Juvenal replies that if it is not safe to attack the living, he will write against the dead.

"securus licet Aenean Rutulum ferocem
committas, nulli gravis est percussus Achilles
aut multum quaesitus Hylas urnamque secutus:
ense velut stricto quoties Lucilius ardens
infremuit, rubet auditor cui frigida mens est
criminibus, tacita sudant praecordia culpa.
inde irae et lacrimae. tecum prius ergo voluta
haec animo ante tubas. galeatum sero duelli
paenitet." experiar quid concedatur in illos
quorum Flaminia tegitur cinis atque Latina.   [162-71]

["It's safe to match Aeneas against the fierce Rutulus. Wounded Achilles is not obnoxious to anybody, or the much-sought-after Hylas who followed the pitcher. But when Lucilius cries out with his drawn sword, the listener whose mind is chilled with crime blushes and his silent innards sweat guilt. Hence anger and tears. It'd be better to turn these things over in the mind carefully before the trumpet sounds. Once the helmet is donned it is too late for regretting the fight." I shall do what is permitted against those whose ashes are covered by the Flaminian and Latin Ways.]

As in Rochester's Imitation, Dryden enters in the role of Lucilius, but for Wood he represents not poetic incompetence, but (as in Pope later) the courageous explicit satirist, whose example Wood, unlike Juvenal, is not afraid to follow, in spite even of the Rose Alley attack, in which a gang of thugs—supposedly hired by Rochester—beat Dryden severely.

Let Puny wits some *Heroe's* fate rehearse,
And *murder* him again in Hobling verse:
My soul this Cowdardice doth wisely Dread,
Tis Cruelty to *cut* and *slash* the Dead.
See our Fam'd *Laureats* frown does fright the Croud,
All fly the vengeance of an angry God.
Their Guilt and Shame an Horrour does express,

Devoutly to him they their *sins* confess.
Perhaps at last, if Wine their Courage move,
With base *Rose-Alley* Drubs they him reprove,
And stand like Capaneus *defying* Jove.
All this *I'le* bear, this I can eas'ly pass,
And boldly march the Muses *Hudibras.*
Be still then *Westminster*, thy Tombs shall rest,
Sleep on ye Reverend Shades in silence Drest.
LONDON, thou sink of Vice, my Stripes expect,
The World shall know, that I the *Living* dare CORRECT.

[pp. 29-30]

It seems that Wood would say anything rather than throw away
a painfully excogitated rhyme or an adverb required *causa metri*,
else why would the guilty "Devoutly . . . confess" their misdeeds
to Dryden—maybe because satirists as torturers, as in the final
couplet, and physicians were already ubiquitous in seventeenth-
century satire and Wood hoped to achieve immortality by inventing a new image, the satirist as confessor. The allusion to the
enemies of Dryden as Capaneus (one of the seven against Thebes)
about to be struck by Dryden wielding the thunderbolt of Jove
is also very odd. Dryden, of course, was quite severely battered
by the attack. Perhaps, as the italics seem to indicate, the allusion
is a quotation and if we knew the original context we should see
the point. In the last couplet Wood gives us not Juvenal himself,
playing safe and writing against the dead, but the Restoration ideal
of the Juvenalian satirist. Wood says of the change: "*Juvenal* here
has thought good to cantradict [*sic*] what he said when he was first
alive [that is, in the original], and Resolves now to prosecute the
Living, as heretofore he did the *Dead.* Tis an easie thing, and very
natural to take an hint from a Place, and raise up its Contrary; the
definition of Imitation does allow of it" (F1v). Not that Wood
was relying for his safety on the definition of Imitation—zealous
secret policemen and informers have little respect for literary
genres. But in 1683 the Tories were in the ascendancy and living
Whigs were quite safe targets. Yet if Wood had been able to write
better verse, *Juvenalis Redivivus* would indeed have brought

Juvenal back to life, as every satirist wishes, on the winning side. Oldham excelled at using Juvenal for social satire, but Wood is the first to turn him loose extensively on contemporary political and literary figures. It is a shame that Wood's Imitation is not more accessible to historians of satire.

Versions of the Late Eighties and Early Nineties

[I]

Although we can easily assign the pecularities of Wood's versification to inadvertence, no such excuse is available to Henry Higden, who created eccentric versions of the thirteenth and tenth satires with his eyes open as he tried to find a compromise between translation and Imitation. Hidgen was trying to solve a real problem. He wanted to avoid *both* literal translation, which sounds quaint and foreign and requires elaborate notes to be comprehensible, *and* Imitation, with its anachronistic contemporary references. In *A Modern Essay on the Thirteenth Satire of Juvenal* (1686), Higden explained to his patron, Lord Dartmouth, the significance of the title.

A Modern Essay Let it be; for as a *Translation* I could not, and as a *Paraphrase* I would not own it: If I have ventured at something between both, I hope I may be the less censured, since the Vices here taxed by our Satyrist, are not so antiquated, but a slight Inquisition may discover them amongst ourselves, though perhaps something altered in Dress and Fashion. As near therefore as I could, I have equipped them Al-a-mode; though nevertheless you'd find little other than the *Old Shock new Trim'd*, and that our present Age comes not much behind our Author's in all sorts of Genteel Vice and Debauchery. . . . (b2r, italics reversed)

"Modern" had not, of course, yet acquired its present sense of all that is desirable and excellent, but it indicates that Higden saw his task as making Juvenal acceptable to contemporary taste, just as "Essay" shows that he was not quite sure how to go about it, and regarded his translation as an experiment, in which he would avoid wholly changing the setting, as Oldham and Wood had done, but would introduce contemporary allusions where they seemed appropriate, as Fanshawe and Brome had done with Horace.

But the feature of Higden's translation that most strikes the reader encountering it for the first time is not the treatment of topicalities and allusions, but the burlesque style to which he reduced Juvenal's elevated Latin. Apparently Higden found his model in Samuel Butler's *Hudibras*.

Juvenal himself sometimes burlesques epic in the thirteenth satire, as when he describes how in the Golden Age there were fewer gods and goddesses and how they lived in frugal simplicity.

nulla super nubes convivia caelicolarum
nec puer Iliacus formosa nec Herculis uxor
ad cyathos, et iam siccato nectare tergens
bracchia Vulcanus Liparaea nigra taberna;
prandebat sibi quisque deus, nec turba deorum
talis ut est hodie ...   [42-47]

[Above the clouds there were no banquets of the dwellers in heaven, nor the Trojan boy and the beautiful wife of Hercules as cupbearers, nor Vulcan wiping his arms blackened from the Liparian workshop after draining his nectar. Each god dined at home and there was no such horde of gods as there is today.]

Here Higden's jaunty octosyllabic meter comes very close to Juvenal's irreverent tone:

The frugal Gods and eke Goddesses
Din'd privately on homely Messes;
Scant Bills of Fare serv'd mod'rate wishes,
Plain wholesome, no Luxurious Dishes.
There Godships in the Upper House
Were not as now so numerous,
When for good Husbandry the Skies
Where manag'd by few Deities.   [p. 10]

But Juvenal's diction, with its epic expressions such as "caelicolarum" and paraphrastic references to Ganymede and Hebe, resembles more the mock-epic style of *MacFlecknoe* than the burlesque style of *Hudibras*. Yet I think he would have been amused by the ridiculous effect of the feminine endings "Goddesses" and "Messes" and the pun on "Upper House" that turns Olympus into the House of Lords.

When, however, Juvenal relies on dignity, restraint, compression, and force, Higden sounds silly. Take Juvenal's argument that because even the criminal who only intended to commit the crime is already guilty, the one who succeeds in his attempt will feel excruciating remorse.

nam scelus intra se tacitum qui cogitat ullum,
facti crimen habet; cedo, si conata peregit:
perpetua anxietas nec mensae tempore cessat,
faucibus ut morbo siccis interque molares
difficili crescente cibo. . . .[1]   [209-13]

[Indeed, anyone who plans a secret crime in his heart is guilty of the deed: what if, let's say, he carries it out? His constant uneasiness doesn't stop at dinner time as like a sick man he finds his food sticks in his dry throat and between his teeth.]

Higden must have despaired of equaling Juvenal's epigrammatic brevity and let himself go, deciding perhaps with Oldham that such excellent sentiments ought to be instilled at length.

Whoever but designs a Crime,
Is guilty, at the self same time,
Altho perhaps he ne'er proceeds
To ripen his intent to Deeds;
If the foul Crime he perpetrate,
Perpetual horrors on him wait;
Th'Effects of black Despair he feels
That haunt and dog him at the heels;
Grief, Sorrow, each unwelcom Guest,
Take Lodgings in his anxious Breast:
If to divert his Pangs he try

Choice Musick, Mirth or Company,
Like Bancoe's Ghost, his ugly Sin,
To marr his Jollity, stalks in;
At Costly Banquet, 'twill not cease
To haunt, and to disturb his peace;
And tho the chief Guest at the Treat
He nauseats all, and cannot eat,
The Morsel chew'd he cannot swallow,
As if his Teeth were clog'd with Tallow.   [pp. 45-46]

Oldham had introduced ghosts to the thirteenth satire, but Higden should get credit (if that is the right word) for being the first to supply Shakespearean allusions to represent the terrors of a mind diseased. Higden must have been proud of his Shakespearean accomplishments, for he inserted another allusion, to describe the malefactor's nightmare.

Bath'd in cold Sweats he frighted Shreiks
At Visions bloodier than King *Dick*'s.   [p. 47]

Reading such passages, and they are typical, we are tempted to ask whether Higden was seriously attempting to translate what he thought Juvenal was saying, or whether he was trying to write a travesty, like Charles Cotton's *Scarronides* or Buckingham's *The Rehearsal*. It would be tempting to argue that Higden anticipated modern critics in interpreting the thirteenth satire as a false consolation, and that he wanted to make fun of its facile and cynical morality.[2] But contemporary readers seem to have taken Higden's translation quite seriously, and so, it appears, did Higden himself. The next year he published a translation entitled *A Modern Essay on the Tenth Satire*, written in the same style, with front matter containing congratulatory poems by Dryden, Aphra Behn, and Elkanah Settle, who had trimmed his sails to the political winds and in 1683 became a Tory. All of them praise Higden's style. Dryden remarked, "This Way took *Horace* to reform an Age."[3] As in the translation of the thirteenth satire, Higden equipped this effort with a full text of the original at the foot of the page, including Latin notes taken from Eilhard Lubin's commentary and at the end fairly elaborate English notes explaining Juvenal's allusions. It is not easy for me to believe that any parodist would go to so much trouble to supply such abundant apparatus; and I am inclined to take the contemporary evidence at face value and conclude that Higden really believed that he was translating Juvenal, albeit into an unusual idiom.

His style is not always as badly suited to the tenth satire as we might expect. When Juvenal resorts to broad strokes of ridicule, Higden, unlike many translators of Juvenal, really is funny, as when the statue of Sejanus is destroyed:

iam stridunt ignes, iam follibus atque caminis
ardet adoratum populo caput et crepat ingens
Seianus: deinde ex facie toto orbe secunda
fiunt urceoli, pelves, sartago, matellae.   [61-64]

[Now the fires crackle, now the bellows and forges burn the head adored by the people and the great Sejanus crackles: from his face, second in all the world, come jugs, basins, a frying pan, and pisspots.]

Higden catches the magnificent anticlimax of "ingens Seianus" becoming "matellae" and the alliterative effects—"ardet adoratum" and, crackling like the fire itself, "caput et crepat"—with his own anticlimactic doggerel, creating a burlesque metamorphosis.

The Founders Fournace grows red hot,
Sejanus Statue goes to pot:
That Head lately ador'd and reckond
In all the Universe the Second,
Melted new forms and shapes assumes,
Of Pisspots, Frying-pans, and Spoons.   [p. 13]

Even better is Higden's version of the folly of wishing for a long life, where Juvenal's account of the loss of all physical pleasures, especially sex, is more detailed than some critics would like.

... nam coitus iam longa oblivio; vel si
coneris, iacet exiguus cum ramice nervus,
et, quamvis tota palpetur nocte, iacebit.
anne aliquid sperare potest haec inguinis aegri
canities? quid, quod merito suspecta libido est,
quae venerem adfectat sine viribus? ...   [204–8]

[For sex has long been forgotten; or if you try, the little member lies down, and though bumped up and down all night, continues to lie down. For what is the old age of a sick groin able to hope for? What indeed, because desire that attempts sex without the ability is rightly suspect.]

In *The Vanity of Human Wishes* Johnson substitutes an elegant but very general precis, "And Luxury with Sighs her Slave resigns" (266), which probably would strike some palates as an improvement. But Juvenal wanted to make old age disgusting and ridiculous, not because he lacked normal human feelings (though Cicero's *De Senectute* is most unusual among classical works in portraying old age as a blessing—anybody who assumes "youth cult" a modern invention ought to read the Greek Anthology and Horace), but because his moral requires that we see as vividly as the satirist can make us that a life prolonged beyond our ability to enjoy it is the worst possible fate.[4] The Hudibrastic style is an ideal medium for Juvenal's tone of detached and amused contempt.

Nor Beauty moves, nor Cupids dart:
Forgetfulness has seiz'd that part,
Long since he there has beeen bewitcht,
'Tis a longe Age since last he itcht.
Obsequious hand cannot excite
The bafled Craven to the fight;
From hoary loynes, and sapless trunk,
In vain strives the industrious punk,
To raise the nerve quite num'd and shrunk.
In *Limberhams*, if *Will* survive,
The impotents new ways contrive;
Having exhausted Natures source
To filthy arts will have recourse.   [pp. 35–36]

Limberham is the appropriately named hero of Dryden's sex comedy *The Kind Keeper*. The allusion is typical of Higden's usual practice when translating. Unlike in the full-fledged Imitation, where the original setting and characters are replaced) in Higden's "modern essays" the major characters and allusions remain classical, but Higden introduces modern examples in place of some of the minor personalities and locations. Rabelais replaces Democritus, Boeotia becomes "Goatham" and Mall Hinton (a whore frequently mentioned in the satires of the 1680s) is Juvenal's Maura. The result of such inconsistency should be an uncouth and particolored translation unable to make up its mind whether it is Roman or English. But I find it quite effective. Higden conveys Juvenal's immediacy and topicality without giving us an entirely new poem, and the anachronisms seem no more bothersome than those constantly perpetrated by biblical translators, for example, Tyndale's apostles who set forth after the Easter holidays.

Was Dryden's praise of Higden sincere? Perhaps. By 1687 Dryden's version of the satires of Juvenal and Persius was already under way, and Dryden must have been thinking hard about what he should do with those pesky allusions that keep sending readers of Juvenal to the commentary.[5] If we allow for the differences between the octosyllabic couplet and its much more elevated decasyllabic brother, many of Dryden's solutions seem remarkably similar to Higden's. In one sense Higden's "modern essays" are among the more eccentric renderings of Juvenal that ever appeared; in another they are directly in the mainstream that leads to the "Augustan mode" of translation.

[II]

Between the publication of Higden's translations of the thirteenth and of the tenth satires a much more literal work intervened, another attempt at the tenth satire, by Thomas Shadwell. Apparently Higden had shown Shadwell his translation, but whatever inspiration Higden supplied, Shadwell disclaimed any aspirations to set up as a rival. In his dedication to Sir Charles Sedley, he said that Higden's version was "in other *Numbers*, and a different *way*, so that we shall not interfere one upon another."[6] But Higden was not mollified and thought he had been made to play Esau to Shadwell's Jacob, remarking in the preface to his version of the tenth satire, in which Shadwell is mentioned specifically, that "the Younger Brother has by the Common-Mother the press outstript the Elder" (a3v). The dedication reveals some other motives for publishing a translation. Shadwell was not pleased with Dryden's portrait of him in *MacFlecknoe*, and Shadwell objected to Dryden's "giving me the *Irish* name of *Mack*, when he knows I never saw *Ireland* till I was three and twenty years old, and was there but four Months" (5:292), an argument so literal-minded that one begins to think that Dryden was right in having Shadwell "confirm'd in full Stupidity." Shadwell was also sensitive to aspersions upon his classical attainments, which may be the reason for his choosing a very close mode of translation; translators, like schoolboys, are often suspected of using free translation to disguise their ignorance.[7]

As may be expected from a writer of his genius, Shadwell is at his worst in the elevated and sententious passages. Higden singled out for ridicule Shadwell's attempt at "cantabit vacuus coram latrone viator" (the empty traveler will sing face to face with the thief, 22):

While the poor man void of all precious things
In Company with Thieves jogg's on and Sings.

[5:298, original italics]

(Shadwell's "jogg's" has become even funnier today, as we imagine the poor traveler kitted out in shorts and running shoes.) In translating the most famous maxim in the tenth satire, Shadwell ignores Juvenal's syntax and enjambs the *sententia*, which ought to stand out.

Pray for a healthful body, a sound mind
That's never to the fear of death inclined,
Which bravely can all toyl and pain surmount,
And Death 'mongst Natures benefits account.

[5:320, original italics]

But where Juvenal is humorous or sarcastic, Shadwell is in his natural element, as when Juvenal gives us the whispers passing through the crowd inspecting the corpse of Sejanus.

... "quae labra, quis illi
vultus erat! numquam, si quid mihi credis, amavi
hunc hominem." "sed quo cecidit sub crimine? quisnam
delator quibus indicibus, quo teste probavit?"
"nil horum; verbosa et grandis epistula venit
a Capreis." "bene habet, nil plus interrogo.". ...   [67-72]

["What lips, what a face that man had! I never—if you ever believe anything I say—liked him." "But for what crime did he perish? Who was the accuser and who were the witnesses? By whose testimony was the charge proved?" "By none of these. A long windy letter came from Capri." "That's fine. I'll ask no more."]

Shadwell remains at once close and idiomatic, perhaps the finest of the translator's accomplishments and one rarely displayed.

Bless me what ugly *blabber-lipps* had he!
A hanging look! and, if you'l credit me,
This fellow I could never once abide.
Can you tell pray for what great crime he dyed?
Who the *Informer?* who the *Evidence?*
What *Ouvert Act?* what proof of his Offence?
None, none of these, but a long Letter sent
From *Capreae*, full of words and Eloquent.
'Tis well, I shall enquire no more. ...   [5:302]

Unfortunately, such passages are scarce. In Shadwell's original satires, such as *The Medal of John Bayes*, a satire on Dryden, he uses the style of old-fashioned "satyr" as practiced by Marston and the Elizabethan satirists and by Restoration authors of political lampoons. It was hardly a suitable style for Juvenal, especially for the tenth satire with its calculated rhetorical effects. In the dedication, Shadwell defended his practice as a translator: "I have alwaies chosen rather to make a rough Verse, than to loose the Sense of *Juvenal*. Tho I must needs say, I do not think great smoothness is required in a *Satyr*, which ought to have a *severe* kind of *roughness* as most fit for *reprehension*, and not that gentle *smoothness* which is necessary to *insinuation*" (5:293). Shadwell, clearly, is reasoning in a circle. Not that this kind of critical thinking went out of fashion in the seventeenth century. The argument that because a work belongs to a certain literary genre or was written in a particular historical period, then it must display the characteristics current literary theory associates with the genre or period, exerts, and will continue to exert, the same mysterious power over literary critics that the Sirens had over sailors. Like the confusion between *satire* and *satyrs* that engendered the notion, the association between rough satire and rough verse died hard. It blinded Shadwell, and many other translators, to the obvious fact that although Juvenal is indeed *rougher* on his targets than Horace, the pedestrian style of Horace was much *rougher* than the elevated style of epic and tragedy employed by Juvenal.

[III]

Shadwell did not mention his real motive for wanting to make Latin satire accessible to English readers: he needed the money. The merger of the Lincoln's Inn and Drury Lane playhouses into the United Company created a theatrical monopoly that destroyed the market for new plays, and the reign of James II was an unauspicious time for an original satirist of Shadwell's "True Blue Protestant" religious and political persuasion. This plight was not unremarked by the young poet Matthew Prior.

Some Poets I confess, the Stage has fed,
Who for Half-crowns are shown, for two pence read;
But these not envy thou, nor imitate,
But rather Starve in *Shadwell*'s silent Fate
Than new vamp Farces, and be Damn'd with *Tate*.   [179-83]

It is strange that there have not been many more Imitations like Prior's *Satyr on the Poets: In Imitation of the Seventh Satire of Juvenal* (1687).[8] Juvenal's complaint against the poor rewards of following literary pursuits would seem a natural candidate for translation from Subura to Grub Street. In the seventh satire Juvenal included the sad lot not only of poets and dramatists, but also of historians, orators, and teachers of literature. Solely interested in poets, Prior used only the first 97 verses as the basis for a 218-line Imitation. He had plenty of space for free expansion. The passage just quoted was inspired by one verse: "haud tamen invideas vati quem pulpita pascunt" (Don't envy the poet whom the stage feeds, 93). This kind of very free adaptation, with no real attempt at keeping a running parallel between the original and the Imitation, reminds one of Rochester and Scroope rather than of Oldham and Wood, whose stricter and more sophisticated technique gives the reader the additional pleasure of seeing the interplay between the original and the Imitation. (Indeed, reading an Imitation with the orignal on the verso, such as the Twickenham Edition of Pope's *Imitations of Horace*, is very like watching a tennis match.)

In the original, Juvenal begins with a flattering address to the emperor, probably Hadrian, insisting that only imperial patronage can relieve the wretched state of literary studies.

Et spes et ratio studiorum in Caesare tantum
solus enim tristes hac tempestate Camenas
respexit, cum iam celebres notique poetae
balneolum Gabiis, Romae conducere furnos
temptarent, nec foedum alii nec turpe putarent
praecones fieri, cum desertis Aganippes
vallibus esuriens migraret in atria Clio.

[Both the hope and the stimulus for literary studies lie in Caesar alone. Only he has looked favorably on the current sad state of the muses, when the most famous and familiar poets try to manage the public baths in Gabia and bakeries in Rome, while others do not find it degrading to become auctioneers, and hungry Clio removes from the deserted valleys of Aganippe into the sale room.]

Prior's target is different from Juvenal's, not the poor wages poets receive, but the poor poets themselves. Prior begins by telling his patron, Lord Dorset:

All my Endeavours, all my Hopes depend
On you, the Orphans and the Muses Friend:
The only great good Man, who will declare
Virtue and Verse the Objects of your care,
And prove a Patron in the worst of times:
When Hungry *Bayes* forsakes his empty Rhymes,
Beseeching all true Catholicks Charity
For a poor Proselyte, that long did lye
Under the Mortal Sins of Verse and Heresie.

Like Rochester, Prior begins his attack with Dryden, who had
converted to Roman Catholicism—opportunistically Protestants
thought—after the ascension to the throne of James II. The *Satyr
on the Poets* must have been written before the publication of
Dryden's theological verse allegory *The Hind and the Panther* but
after the incredibly dreary apologetical treatise in prose called *A
Defence of the Papers* appeared, so that it seemed that Dryden had
abandoned poetry for theology. In the next verse paragraph Prior
turns to attack Shadwell, Nahum Tate, Settle, and Thomas
Durfey, noting that "Poets of all Religions are the same" (11). We
soon notice that Prior's methods are quite different from Rochester's, that although the *Satyr on the Poets* is like "An Allusion to
Horace" in being a literary satire, it is more like Pope's *Dunciad*
in making the poverty of contemporary poets the object of the
satirist's scorn. The flattery lavished on Dorset, who had been
responsible for Prior's education and advancement, is scarcely
excessive in an age when flattery was a recognized art form. But
the attempt to turn the poor rewards enjoyed by one's fellow
authors into an encomium on one's patron is unusual and unset-
tling.

Juvenal said only the emperor would give enough patronage to
revive the arts—doubtless an example of the wish being father to
the thought—and castigates the meanness and vanity of all other
contemporary patrons. In contrast, Prior deserts his original to set
up an opportunity to lavish some more flattery on Dorset. He has
an interlocutor interrupt to complain that Prior is contradicting
himself by writing a poem damning the vocation of poet. There

is nothing wrong with writing poetry, Prior replies, so long as one has a generous patron.

True Sir, I write, and have a Patron too,
To whom my Tributary Songs are due;
Yet with your leave I'de honestly dissuade
Those wretched Men from *Pindus* barren Shade:
Who, tho they tire their Muse and rak their Brains,
With blustring Heroes, and with piping Swains,
Can no Great patient giving Man engage
To fill their Pockets and their Title Page.   [42-49]

Juvenal's sympathies are with the poet of real ability who cannot gain a decent living from his poetry because stingy patrons will not recognize and reward merit except with cheap praise.

frange miser calamum vigilataque proelia dele
qui facis in parva sublimia carmina cella,
ut dignus venias hederis et imagine macra.
spes nulla ulterior; didicit iam dives avarus
tantum admirari, tantum laudare disertos,
ut pueri Iunonis avem. . . .   [27-32]

[Wretch, break your pen and scratch out the epic you spent your nights toiling over, you who make sublime poems in a little garret so that you might become worthy of the ivy and a gaunt bust. There is no further hope; the rich miser knows only to admire, only to praise accomplished poets, as boys do the bird of Juno (the peacock).]

But Prior's neglected poets deserve the neglect they have received, destined for the used-book stall to be hawked alongside illustrated ballads.

But on; your ruin stubbornly pursue;
Herd with the hungry little Chiming Crew,
Obtain the empty Title of a Wit,
And be a free-cost Noisie in the Pit,
Print your dull Poems, and before 'em place
A Crown of Laurel, and a Meager Face:

And may just Heav'n thy hated Life prolong,
'Till thou blest Author! See'st thy deathless Song
The dusty Lumber of a *Smithfield* Stall
And find thy Picture starch'd to Suburb Wall,
With *Jony Armstrong*, and the Prodigal.   [57-67]

Not even Pope, I think, ever suggests that "just Heav'n" keeps the dunces alive to punish them by making sure that they know they are failures. But the artistic snobbery implicit in the notion that writers who cannot find a patron like Dorset and have to depend on the public deserve a life of penury, is somewhat mitigated by the satiric interlocutor, who describes the kind of bad patron who recognizes artistic merit when he sees it, but is too mean to reward it. Like Juvenal, the interlocutor is galled by the freedom the wealthy amateur enjoys to indulge his own tastes and to write for posterity, "contentus fama iaceat Lucanus in hortis / marmoreis" (let Lucan lie content with fame in his marble garden, 79-80), or to amuse his friends—"*Sidley* indeed and *Rochester* might Write, / For their own Credit, and their Friends Delight" (145-46). But the poor professional must write what will sell. Juvenal's example was Statius, best known as the author of the *Thebaid*—an epic now regarded as a windy collection of rhetorical conceits—although Chaucer and the young Pope loved it—who had to write for the stage to survive. (Juvenal furnishes our only evidence that Statius ever wrote plays.)

curritur ad vocem iucundam et carmen amicae
Thebaidos, laetam cum fecit Statius urbem
promisitque diem; tanta dulcedine captos
adficit ille animos tantaque libidine volgi
auditur; sed cum fregit subsellia versu,
esurit, intactam Paridi nisi vendit Agaven.   [82-87]

[They run to the happy voice and the poem, the beloved *Thebaid*, when Statius has made the city happy and promised the day; he fills the captured minds of the crowd with delight and is heard with pleasure; but when he has shattered the benches with his verses, he starves, unless he can sell a pristine (that is, unacted role of) *Agave* to Paris (an actor who enjoyed political patronage).]

Prior turns the screw a little further, describing not the epic poet who has to turn to the stage to survive—Dryden would be a good example—but a popular dramatic writer who quite literally was starved to death by the same theatrical monopoly that forced Shadwell to try to set up as a translator.

There was a time When *Otway* Charm'd the Stage;
Otway the Hope, and Sorrow of our Age!
When the full Pitt with pleas'd attention hung,
Wrap'd with each Accent from *Castalio's* Tongue:
With what a Laughter was his Soldier read!
How Mourn'd they, when his *Jaffier* Struck and Bled!
Yet this best Poet, tho with so much ease,
He never drew his Pen, but sure to please:
Tho Lightning were less lively than his Wit,
And Thunder-claps less loud than those o'th' Pit,
He had of's many Wants, much earlier dy'd,
Had not kind Banker *Betterton* supply'd,
And took for Pawn, the Embrio of a Play,
Till he could pay himself the next Third-day.   [155-69]

The "Soldier" was Thomas Otway's comedy *The Souldier's Fortune* and Jaffeir the hero of *Venice Preserved*, one of the few Restoration tragedies that anybody besides experts on later seventeenth-century drama ever bothers to read. Playwrights received the profits from the third (and if they had what was then a hit, the sixth and ninth) day; if the play folded after the first or second day the author received nothing. If anything, a Restoration dramatist seems to have been worse off than playwrights in Juvenal's time.

Prior ends his poem with a panegyric on his patron, begging Dorset to take "The little Offering a poor Muse can make" and apologizing that a "Muse so Young" could not inspire the praise such a patron deserves.

Yet Vows her Labor She'l one day renew,
With Strengthn'd Wings the glorious Toil Pursue;
And Sing of wondrous Piety and You.   [216-18]

I find the *Satyr on the Poets* both a poor Imitation of Juvenal's seventh satire and unattractive as an original poem. The seventh satire depends for its effect on Juvenal's favorite theme, the abuse rich patrons heap on poor clients, whether it is making them listen to bad poetry, bolt bad dinners, sodomize the patron, or impregnate his wife. Prior confuses us by trying to write satire and panegyric simultaneously, so that we hear Prior, the amateur poet with the generous patron, Dorset (whose presence is only warranted by Juvenal's opening address to Hadrian), as well as the satiric interlocutor, who represents the authentic voice of the Juvenalian satirist as he attempts to arouse Prior's sympathy for neglected and unrewarded poets. Perhaps we can begin to see why Imitations of the seventh satire were not more common in the seventeenth and eighteenth centuries (though I suspect it lies behind the career of the young scholar in Johnson's *The Vanity of Human Wishes*); it is not the sort of poem a poor poet would want to dedicate to a patron, or that a financially secure poet would find a congenial subject. It is easy to understand why Prior, so greatly obliged to Dorset, should go out of his way to dissociate his patron from the kind Juvenal attacked, and to depict himself as a wonderful exception to the general lot of poets. But to do it he has to turn Juvenal inside out, making a hero of the wealthy patron and scorning the fate of the poor poet. A mature Prior might have done better by Juvenal (indeed *Solomon or the Vanity of the World* could be regarded as an elephantine tenth satire), but I doubt that any of his admirers could regard the disappearance of the Juvenalian satirist and the emergence of the Horatian lyricist as much of a loss to the muses.

[IV]

The year 1687 would have been even richer in new versions of Juvenal if *The Tenth Satyr of Juvenal Done into English Verse* had been published when its author, "J. H. Esq." (apparently John Harvey), had wished.[9] In the dedication Harvey says that he composed the translation in 1683, and when he heard that a new translation of Juvenal was being planned sent a copy to Dryden's bookseller Jacob Tonson. Harvey adds that "no notice in the least [was] taken of this by Mr. *Dryden,* who perhaps possibly might not see it, altho' his Bookseller had it for five years by him, and still has it or lost it" (A4v). Yet Harvey did not complain that Dryden plagiarized from him; rather that when the volume appeared with Dryden's version of the tenth satire instead of his, a friend told him he ought to publish it lest "several of your Acquaintance [who] have expected it, and who only having heard of it, will think it worse than it is."

That would be hard to do. Harvey continually wobbles on the brink of the ridiculous, notwithstanding the high esteem in which he held the moral qualities of the tenth satire: "I do not recollect I ever read any thing (except in Holy Writ) which contains such comprehensive Benefit in such short Dimensions, and affords such a variety of Matter for Divines to handle more at large from their Pulpits" (B1r).[10] Whatever was confusing or obscure in Juvenal's Latin comes out equally so in Harvey's English. For example, when Juvenal warns that any kind of excessive power — civil power, military power, power of speaking, or even muscle power — is dangerous

. . . nocitura toga, nocitura petuntur
militia; torrens dicendi copia multis
et sua mortifera est facundia; viribus ille
confisus periit admirandisque lacertis. [8-11]

[. . . the deadly toga and deadly military command are sought; a torrential abundance of speech and their own eloquence are fatal to many; that man, stuck, perished on account of his strength and amazing muscles.]

Harvey, like Wood, will say anything to rhyme.

Perils proceed not from the Sword alone,
As fatal Dangers do attend the Gown;
And many a Man his Death has fondly met
By's florid Tongue and overflowing Wit;
He too, who made a God of his strong Arms
Trusting to them, from them he felt his harms. [p. 2]

For the reader who might wonder who the strong man was, Harvey is a mine of information presented in a strangely collo-quial style: ". . . all persons agree this man here meant to be *Milo* of *Crotana*, who was a devilish strong huffing Fellow: He would carry an Ox a Furlong, and hold his Breath all the while: He would knock down a Bull stark Dead, with one blow of his Fist, and afterwards make but one meals Meat of him. At last striving to rend an Oak in two, his Arms were caught in the Cleft of it, and there he was held till some wild Beasts in Revenge came and devoured him" (p. 19). Often Harvey introduces English parallels in his notes. Ulbrae, a proverbial ghost town, is "a little better than *Castle Rising*, and not quite so good as *Higham-Ferrars* in *North-amptonshire*," two notorious rotten boroughs. Mark Antony was "a bloody Roman Tory" (*that* note must have been written after 1688), and Themison the incompetent doctor, "an Eminent Phy-sician in *Rome*, famous there as *Willis* or *Lower* amongst us of late, and killed as many perhaps." Unlike the modern scholar obsessed with documentation, fortunately Harvey knew when to stop. Hamillus, the schoolmaster who buggered his pupils, is described simply as "a filthy Sodomite," and of Lucretia Harvey is content to remark, "Ravish'd by *Sextus Tarquinius*. The Story is known sufficiently."

Like Higden, Harvey is at his best when Juvenal is most scornful, as in the account of Alexander the Great that demon-strates what a contemptible thing is miltary glory.

unus Pellaeo iuveni non sufficit orbis;
aestuat infelix angusto limite mundi
ut Gyarae clausus scopulis parvaque Seripho:
cum tamen a figulis munitam intraverit urbem,
sarcophago contentus erit. mors sola fatetur
quantula sint hominum corpuscula . . .   [168-73]

[One world was not enough for the Macedonian youth; unhappy, he was irritated by the narrow limits of the world as if shut up in the rocks of Gyara or tiny Seriphus. Yet when he had entered the city walled with brick, he was satisfied with a sarcophagus. Only death shows what tiny things are the little bodies of men.]

In Harvey's version:

The great *Pellaean* Youth complains, and cries,
One World's too narrow for my Victories;
This Earth wants elbow room, as if the while,
H'had been Coop't up in Rocky *Gyarus* Isle:
Yet having enter'd *Babylon*, we see,
A Coffin held him wondrous quietly.
Death shews what Human Composition is
He's the Plain-dealer of our Carkasses.   [p. 10]

"A Coffin held him wondrous quietly" has the sound of a line from a Jacobean tragedy, though "Plain-dealer of our Carkasses" may try too hard for effect.

It is unclear why Harvey kept the obscure "Pellaean" (the name of a mountain in Macedonia) but changed "the city fortified with brick" to the simple "*Babylon*"; although the reason Alexander "cries" is easy to discover—Harvey needed the rhyme.

The translation has some good earthy language in other places too; Hannibal is the "one-eye'd Spark" ("ducem . . . luscum") and Xerxes a "blustering Huff" who ordered the winds whipped for blowing the wrong way and delaying his invasion; they were "Never so firk't before by Æolus" ("Aeolio numquam hoc in carcere passos"). Harvey is better than Higden at avoiding indiscriminate burlesque touches, and his pentameter couplets are less jocular than Higden's tetrameters, though not much easier to take seriously as poetry. Why Harvey thought Dryden would need his version is hard to imagine, but at least, like Higden, Harvey shows that not all seventeenth-century readers supposed that Juvenal is always elevated and stately, even in the tenth satire where he rivals Holy Writ.

It is odd that the next example of Juvenal the humorist should come from John Dennis, who was later to characterize Juvenal as a tragic satirist, and who is best known as an advocate of Milton and sacred epic (or perhaps it would be more accurate to say, as Alexander Pope's most irascible and relentless critic). In his Imitation of the eighth satire (only his version of the first fifty-

four verses survives), against degenerate aristocrats, Dennis introduces some low touches of his own, as when Juvenal warns the
haughty nobleman Rubellius that famous ancestors are nothing
to boast about:

> his ego quem monui? tecum est mihi sermo, Rubelli
> Plance. tumes alto Drusorum stemmate, tamquam
> feceris ipse aliquid propter quod nobilis esses,
> ut te conciperet quae sanguine fulget Iuli,
> non quae ventoso conducta sub aggere texit.   [39-43]

[Whom am I warning with these remarks? This conversation is between
you and me, Rubellus Plancus. Though you boast that you came from
the noble line of the Drusi, as if you'd ever done anything yourself to
deserve being a nobleman, just because the woman who conceived you
was distinguished by the blood of Julius rather than being the hired
woman who weaves under the windy embankment.]

Juvenal's mention of Rubellus' mother gave Dennis the inspiration for some coarse fun:

> This let *Rubellius Plancus* ponder well,
> Whom the brave *Drusi*'s lofty Line do's swell.
> As if such Virtues did in *Plancus* shine,
> That (could he yet be got) those Pow'rs Divine,
> Might claim to be incorporate in *Rome*'s Imperial Line:
> As if such *Things* could not in haste be made
> By some lewd Rogue, and some Suburbian Jade.
> Had but his sporting Mother known that *Thing*
> Would from the pleasure which she toyl'd for Spring,
> That very thought had damp'd her active Flame,
> And of approaching Bliss had bilk'd the panting dame.[11]

The triplet is very crabbed; I think it means that if Rubellius really
had the qualities he ascribed to himself, the gods might better
bestow them on the emperor. Dennis's aspersion that had Rubellius' mother known what a blockhead would result from her
amorous activites, she would have lost her enthusiasm, reminds
one more of a court satirist of the time of Charles II than of

Juvenal. Perhaps Juvenal's later comparison of nobles to race-horses (56-67) suggested "the panting Dame" to Dennis. Fortunately, Dennis was a better critic (when not carried away by his hatred of Pope) than he was a translator, and his *To Mr. Prior; upon the Roman Satirists*, remains a locus classicus for seventeenth-century notions of Horatian and Juvenalian satire.

Dryden and His Myrmidons

[I]

Dennis's translation of Juvenal's eighth satire is cast in the shade by the great event of 1692, the appearance in November of *The Satires of Decimus Junius Juvenalis. Translated into English Verse. By Mr. Dryden and Several Other Eminent Hands* (title page dated 1693), in which the first, third, sixth, tenth, and sixteenth satires were translated by Dryden, who also supplied a long introductory essay—in the form of a dedication to that model of enlightened patrons, the Earl of Dorset—called the "Discourse Concerning the Original and Progress of Satire." This project was to remain the standard English translation of Juvenal for over one hundred years, till William Gifford's version of 1802. I shall not discuss the Original and Progress of Satire, which belongs to the history of criticism, not of translation and adaption of classical satire. But it contains an important statement of principles, which Dryden said that he and his subordinate translators followed, that deserves quotation in full.

This must be said for our Translation, that if we give not the whole Sense of *Juvenal*, yet we give the most considerable Part of it: We give it, in General, so clearly, that few Notes are sufficient to make us Intelligible: We make our Author at least appear in a Poetique Dress: We have actually made him more Sounding, and more Elegant, than he was before in *English*: And have endeavour'd to make him speak that kind of *English*, which he wou'd have spoken had he liv'd in *England*, and Written to this Age. If sometimes any of us (and 'tis but seldome) make him express the Customs and Manners of our Native Country, rather than of *Rome;* 'tis, either when there was some kind of Analogy, betwixt their Customes and ours; or when, to make him more easy to Vulgar Understandings, we gave him those Manners which are familiar to us. But I defend not this Innovation, 'tis enough if I can excuse it. For to speak sincerely, the Manners of Nations and Ages, are not to be confounded: We shou'd either make them *English*, or leave them *Roman.* If this can neither be defended, nor excus'd, let it be pardon'd, at least, because it is acknowledg'd; and so much the more easily, as being a fault which is never committed without some Pleasure to the Reader.

Dryden characterized this method as, "not a Literal Translation, but a kind of Paraphrase; or somewhat which is yet more loose, betwixt a Paraphrase and Imitation."[1] Dryden does not define these terms here, and it is not clear just where the area "betwixt a Paraphrase and Imitation" lies.[2] Perhaps it would be better not to speculate on what Dryden thought he was doing and instead to infer what we can from his practice.

Three elements are characteristic of Dryden's rendering of Juvenal, and to some extent of the work of his assistants. First of all, the basic unit for the translator to reproduce was neither the metrical line of dactylic hexameter (the *verse*) nor the grammatical unit (the *sentence*), but the verse paragraph—a group of related sentences culminating in a point (often a *sententia*). In the original Latin manuscripts, of course, there was no such thing as a paragraph (though they are usually introduced by modern editors) but the same kind of strong stop occurs when the grammatical unit—the period—ends at the same time as the metrical unit—the verse. (The same phenomenon can often be observed in English blank verse, as in the opening sixteen lines of Milton's *Paradise Lost.*) Second, references to particular persons and institutions familiar to Juvenal's audience but not to Dryden's are replaced with more generalized examples (for example, at 1.155, "Tigellinum" is translated "Rogues Omnipotent" [1.234, in Dryden's translation]). Glosses may be introduced into the text to clarify allusions, and when additional information is needed (and sometimes, as we shall see, when it is not) a note is supplied. Modern allusions are sometimes added, even without very much warrant in the Latin, but carefully to avoid obvious anachronisms. Finally and most important, the resources of English versification, couplet dynamics, and poetic diction are fully mobilized and employed vigorously and resourcefully to match Juvenal's elevated epic hexameters.

Take the passage in the first satire in which Juvenal imagines himself standing by the side of the road and boiling with anger as a procession of villains passes by.

quid referam quanta siccum iecur ardeat ira,
cum populum gregibus comitum premit hic spoliator
pupilli prostantis, et hic damnatus inani
iudicio? quid enim salvis infamia nummis?
exul ab octava Marius bibit et fruitur dis
iratis, at tu victrix provincia ploras! [45-50]

[How could I say how much my thirsty liver burns with anger, when the dispoiler of a prostituted ward presses the populace with a herd of retainers, and this one, condemned by a meaningless verdict? What difference does infamy make when the money's safe? The exiled Marius drinks from the eighth hour and enjoys the anger of the gods, but you, victorious province, weep!]

The passage abounds in pitfalls for the translator. It is easy to find suitable inner organs for the liver (which the ancients thought the seat of the emotions), but the compressed cynicism of "quid enim salvis infamia nummis," "fruitur dis iratis" and "victrix provincia ploras"—to depict a society where vice is rewarded and virtue punished—resists translation. And what does one do with Marius, the provincial governor whose successful prosecution by Tacitus and Pliny resulted only in a pleasant retirement to Marseilles, a gastronome's paradise? Dryden evaded most of the traps, though he had to sacrifice impact for clarity.

What Indignation boils within my Veins,
When perjur'd Guardians, proud with Impious Gains,
Choak up the Streets, too narrow for their Trains!
Whose Wards by want betray'd, to Crimes are led
Too foul to Name, too fulsom to be read!

When he who pill'd his Province scapes the Laws,
And keeps his Money though he lost his Cause:
His Fine begg'd off, contemns his Infamy,
Can rise at twelve, and get him Drunk e're three:
Enjoys his Exile, and, Condemn'd in vain,
Leaves thee, prevailing Province, to complain!   [67-77]

It is remarkable how Dryden's metrical ingenuity welds the passage together; the opening triplet links the angry satirist to the "perjur'd Guardians" and the repetition (*anaphora*) "When perjur'd" and "When he" (Juvenal's "hic . . . et hic") connects the guardians with the corrupt governor. Dryden avoids having to explain who Marius was by making him anonymous and brings him up to date by changing him from an epicure³ to a Restoration rake like the Rochester in the satirical poem beginning "I rise at eleven. . . ." Notice too how "he" in line 72 is the subject of the verbs in the next five lines, holding the three couplets together as a grammatical unit, and how in "keeps his Money though he lost his Cause" Dryden uses parallelism and antithesis to preserve some of the epigrammatic crackle of "salvis infamia nummis," even though Dryden could not find a place for "infamia" till the next line in which it appears, considerably weakened, as "contemns his Infamy." Dryden must not have found "prevailing Province" (did he borrow the phrase from Holyday to keep Juvenal's alliterating "provincia ploras"?) clear enough, and added the note: "Here the Poet complains that the Governours of Provinces being accus'd for their unjust Exactions, though they were condemned at their Tryals, yet got off by Bribery" (*Works*, 4:108). If he needed a note anyway, why did Dryden not explain who Marius was? He may have thought that his audience of "Gentlemen and Ladies, who tho they are not Scholars are not Ignorant" (*Works*, 4:87), hardly needed to identify by name an obscure colonial official.

Topical allusions, especially to obscure figures, quickly become impenetrable; many of the identifications in the scholia in the margins of manuscripts of Horace and Juvenal are probably wild guesses by late classical grammarians who had nothing better to do while waiting for the Goths to arrive and get on with the sacking and looting. Even when we can find out tô whom the allusions refer, looking them up in the notes is distracting. So Dryden's decision to put the glosses into the text and to replace specific individuals with general types lets readers concentrate, as they should, on the poetry.

Not that Dryden always resists the urge to enlighten his audience beyond the immediate need to see the satirist's point. Perhaps the funniest example of Dryden's weakness for the otiose occurs in his translation of the third satire, when Juvenal describes the danger of tenement fires.

... tabulata tibi iam tertia fumant:
tu nescis; nam si gradibus trepidatur ab imis
ultimus ardebit quem tegula sola tuetur
a pluvia, molles ubi reddunt ova columbae.   [199-202]

[Now the third floor smokes. You don't even know it. For if the alarm is raised downstairs, the last one the fire will burn will be the one protected only by the tiles from the rain, where the soft doves lay their eggs.]

Dryden seems to have missed Juvenal's point, which is that if you live on the uppermost story you will not hear the cries of alarm and will not discover the fire till it is too late. So he gives his own reason why the sleeper is oblivious to the fire, as well as looking after the birds.

Thy own third Storey smoaks; while thou, supine,
Art drench'd in Fumes of undigested Wine.
For if the lowest Floors already burn,
Cock-lofts and Garrets soon will take the Turn:
Where thy tame Pidgeons next the Tiles were bred
Which in their Nests unsafe, are timely fled.   [326-31]

Animal lovers among Dryden's readers must have been grateful to the translator for contriving at the birds' escape, a detail that Juvenal overlooked. But why did Dryden imagine that the pigeons needed a note also, and go on to tell us: "The *Romans* us'd to breed their tame Pidgeons in their Garrets" (*Works*, 4:143)? Perhaps because Dryden found the ridiculous irresistible, even in such serious works as *Alexander's Feast* and the translation of the first book of the *Iliad*.

When Dryden found the right opportunities for his natural taste in broad ridicule and bathetic humor, he tends to be a little less sharp and witty than Juvenal, but equally funny. The description in the sixth satire of the adulterous wife who is always perfectly groomed for her lover, but who goes to bed with her husband covered with night cream and skin softeners, shows how Dryden handled Juvenal's characteristic hyperbole.

interea foeda aspectu ridendaque multo
pane tumet facies aut pinguia Poppaeana
spirat, et hinc miseri viscantur labra mariti:
ad moechum lota veniunt cute. quando videri
vult formonsa domi? moechis foliata parantur,
his emitur quidquid graciles huc mittitis Indi.
tandem aperit vultum et tectoria prima reponit,
incipit agnosci, atque illo lacte fovetur
propter quod secum comites educit asellas
exul Hyperboreum si dimittatur ad axem.
sed quae mutatis inducitur atque fovetur
tot medicaminibus coctaeque siliginis offas
accipit et madidae, facies dicetur an ulcus?   [461-73]

[Her face is foul and ridiculous to see, swollen with (a face-pack of) bread or reeking with sticky pastes that cling to the lips of her husband, although women go to their lovers with shining skin. When will a woman want to look good at home? They wear perfumes for lovers, for them they buy whatever you slender Indians export. At last her face appears: she takes off the original stucco and begins to be recognizable; she bathes herself with that milk for which she would lead a train of little she-asses with her were she exiled to the Hyperborean pole. But when it is coated and layered with so many cosmetics and lumps of cooked and wet paste, should it be called a face—or an ulcer?]

As readers of *MacFlecknoe* and *Absalom and Achitophel* well

know, couplet satirists delight especially in the stinging anticlimax.

She duely, once a Month, renews her Face;
Mean time, it lies in Dawb, and hid in Grease;
Those are the Husband's Nights; she craves her due,
He takes fat Kisses, and is stuck in Glue.
But, to the Lov'd Adult'rer when she steers,
Fresh from the Bath, in brightness she appears:
For him the Rich *Arabia* sweats her Gum;
And Precious Oyls from distant *Indies* come:
How Haggardly so e're she looks at home.
Th' Eclipse then vanishes; and all her Face
Is open'd, and restor'd to ev'ry Grace.
The Crust remov'd, her Cheeks as smooth as Silk;
Are polish'd with a wash of Asses Milk;
And, shou'd she to the farthest North be sent,
A Train of these attend her Banishment.
But, hadst thou seen her Plaistred up before,
'Twas so unlike a Face, it seem'd a Sore.   [593-609]

The sudden shock of Juvenal's "facies ... an ulcus?" does not
quite come through in Dryden's translation, but Dryden adds
some Juvenalian touches of his own, especially, ". . . she craves her
due, / He takes fat Kisses, and is stuck in Glue." Juvenal would
have been chagrined that he did not think to make the wife—
covered in sticky night cream with her hair bound in papers—the
sexual aggressor.

[II]

Before considering what Dryden's assistants made of Juvenal, we
might take a look at Dryden's version of the satires of Persius,
which was appended to the volume. Dryden must have been
distressed by Persius' delight in uncouth expressions and bizarre
metaphors, which create the general effect, as a friend of mine
once remarked, of lightning striking through fog. But Dryden did
not attempt to translate Persius into the old-fashioned "satyr"

style of Donne and Marston, who had deliberately cultivated Persius' obscurity. Usually Dryden reminds one more of the Horatian translators, such as Oldham, though Dryden sometimes reproduces Persius' "bold" figures, especially when the satirist's point depends on them. In the first satire, Persius describes a poetry recital. These—as anyone who has read Juvenal knows— are among the horrors of life. Persius added another twist by describing an effeminate poet's reading in images of a homosexual orgy, a passage that in Dryden's time was taken to depict the Emperor Nero himself in action.

Scribimus inclusi, numeros ille, hic pede liber,
grande aliquid quod pulmo animae praelargus anhelet.
scilicet haec populo pexusque togaque recenti
et natalicia tandem cum sardonyche albus
sede leges celsa, liquido cum plasmate guttur
mobile conlueris, patranti fractus ocello.
hic neque more probo videas neque voce serena
ingentes trepidare Titos, cum carmina lumbum
intrant et tremulo scalpuntur ubi intima versu.
tun, vetule, auriculis alienis colligis escas,
auriculis quibus et dicas cute perditus "ohe"?   [13-23]

[We write in private, some in verse, some without poetic feet, which comes out of our breathless lungs as something big. And you read this stuff with your hair prettily arranged, in a nice new toga, with a birthday ring, sitting on a high chair with liquid gargle sliding down your deep throat and rolling your eyes. Here you can see famous Roman aristocrats wiggling wantonly and screaming, as the poems are stuck into them, as their innards are tickled by the quivering verse. And do you, you old faggot, cater hors d'oeuvres for other ears, ears to which you ought to say, as you're about to burst, "enough"?]*

Sexual allusions and double entendres are tricky, even for a translator who was "licentious" in both senses of the word, perhaps because sexual slang is usually invented by coarse insensitive people with something on their minds other than the justness of their similes and the exactness of their descriptions.

First, to begin at Home, our Authors write
In lonely Rooms, secur'd from publick sight;
Whether in Prose or Verse, 'tis all the same:
The Prose is Fustian, and the Numbers lame.
All Noise, and empty Pomp, a storm of words,
Lab'ring with sound, that little Sence affords.
They Comb, and then they order ev'ry Hair:
A Gown, or White, or Scour'd to whiteness, wear:
A Birth-day Jewel bobbing at their Ear:
Next, gargle well their Throats; and thus prepar'd,
They mour.t, a God's Name, to be seen and heard
From their high Scaffold; with a Trumpet Cheeck:
And Ogling all their Audience e'er they speak.
The nauseous Nobles, ev'n the Chief of *Rome*,
With gaping Mouths to these Rehearsals come,
And pant with Pleasure, when some lusty line
The Marrow pierces, and invades the Chine.
At open fulsom Bawdry they rejoice;
And slimy Jests applaud with broken Voice.
Base Prostitute, thus dost thou gain thy Bread?
Thus dost thou feed their Ears, and thus art fed?
At his own filthy stuff he grins, and brays;
And gives the sign where he expects their praise.   [29-51]

Now Persius' poet not only represents corrupt literary taste, but homosexual prostitution and Grub street commercialism. (Indeed, a line such as "Lab'ring with sound, that little Sense affords" could have come from *MacFlecknoe.*) Dryden preserves the metaphor of the poem buggering the audience, though the following couplet, "At open fulsom Bawdry they rejoice; / And slimy Jests applaud with broken Voice," seems an expansive gloss intended for a reader too innocent to figure out what is going on. Dryden must have taken "cute perditus" as meaning that the prostitute-poet has run to fat from excessive feasting with his customers (modern editors generally take it as an allusion to dropsy or impotence) and "ohe" as a signal for applause. But Dryden had trouble with the sexual vocabulary. Persius has "patranti fractus ocello"—"fractus" literally means "broken" but probably implies wantonness (like our "loose") and "patranti" literally means "doing" but has the same connotations as our "doing it." Dryden resorts to paraphrase: "And Ogling all their Audience e're they speak." English Augustan poetic practice reverses the normal generic expectation that low words should be used to describe nasty people and things; among the most elevated passages in *MacFlecknoe* and the *Dunciad* are the bathroom jokes. By trying to use proper words in improper places, and carefully avoiding figures ill-paired and similes unlike, Dryden's Persius is prissier than the original.

But Augustan standards of correctness were useful when it came to translating Persius' parodies of corrupt modern style. In the first satire an interlocutor interrupts and exclaims that modernists have made brilliant innovations in technique and style.

"sed numeris decor est et iunctura addita crudis.
cludere sic versum didicit 'Berecyntius Attis'
et 'qui caeruleum dirimebat Nerea delphin,'
sic 'costam longo subduximus Appennino.' "   [92-95]

["But we have added elegance and smoothness to our crude meters. We have learned how to close a verse with 'Berecyntius Attis' or 'the dolphin who was slicing through the sea-blue Nereus,' or 'we have snatched a rib from the long Apennines.' "]

Dryden noted that the quotations were from "Foolish Verses of *Nero*, which the Poet repeats; and which cannot be Translated properly into *English*."[5] So far as we can tell, a word like "Berecyntius" taking up half of the fourth and all of the fifth foot of an hexameter verse would have sounded peculiar to a Roman ear attuned to the Virgilian hexameter of the Golden Age. Similarly, the images of a sea god being dissected by an aquatic mammal and of a mountain being carved like a standing rib roast (as well as the spondaic verse ending "Appennino"), which the modernist regards as examples of the latest literary fashion, would have seemed as odd to a reader of traditional Roman taste as the poetry of, say, John Ashbery does to some of us. Fortunately, the rules of the heroic couplet were nearly as well defined as those for the classical

hexameter; so although Dryden could not duplicate Persius'
effects, he could create some that were equally strange.

> But to raw Numbers, and unfinish'd Verse,
> Sweet sound is added now, to make it Terse:
> " 'Tis tagg'd with Rhyme, like *Berecynthian Atys*,
> The mid part chimes with Art, which never flat is.
> The Dolphin brave, that cut the liquid Wave,
> Or He who in his line, can chine the long-rib'd *Apennine*."
>
> [182–87]

The jingling internal rhymes, anticlimactic feminine endings
("Atys"/"flat is"), impossible end rhymes, and the final fourteen-
syllable line fill the rendition with literary grotesqueries.
Also supposed to be Nero's were some verses Persius ridicules
a bit further on in the first satire, from a poem on the Bacchae.

> "torva Mimalloneis inplerunt cornua bombis,
> et raptum vitulo caput ablatura superbo
> Bassaris et lyncem Maenas flexura corymbis
> euhion ingeminat, reparabilis adsonat echo."   [99–102]

["They filled their grim horns with Mimallonean boomings, and a
Bassarid about to carry off the head torn from a proud calf and a Maenad
about to rein a lynx with ivy branches redouble their ecstatic cry, and
replying echo joins in."]

Here the meter is not particularly eccentric, rather Persius is
satirizing Nero's love of tasteless sensationalism—Nero is describing a group of maenads preparing to tear a calf to pieces with their
bare hands—and his predilection for Grecisms, serious defects in
classical Latin verse. Though in his note on the passage Dryden
calls the verses "mere bombast," he added some metrical per-
culiarities to his strained poetic diction.

> "Their crooked Horns the *Mimallonian* Crew
> With Blasts inspir'd: and *Bassaris* who slew
> The scornful Calf, with Sword advanc'd on high,
> Made from his Neck his haughty Head to fly,

> And *Maenas*, when the Ivy-bridles bound,
> She led the spotted Lynx, then *Evion* rung around;
> *Evion* from Woods and Floods repairing Ecchos sound." [194-200]

Seventeenth-century readers would be surprised indeed to find a triplet concluded with two alexandrines, and a syntactical order that makes it sound as if the calf advanced with the sword and that it was the Maenad who was bound with the ivy bridle. The jingle "Woods and Floods" would have sounded very clumsy, and in Dryden's day was an exact rhyme.

Yet Persius was most esteemed by seventeenth-century readers not as a parodist and literary critic, but as a moralist. As Dryden remarks in the "Discourse":

The Philosophy in which *Persius* was Educated, and which he professes through his whole Book, is the Stoick: The most noble, most generous, most beneficial to Humane Kind, amongst all the Sects, who have given us the Rules of Ethiques, thereby to form a severe Virtue in the Soul; to raise in us an undaunted Courage, against the assaults of Fortune; to esteem as nothing the things that are without us, because they are not in our Power; not to value Riches, Beauty, Honours, Fame, or Health, any farther than as conveniences, and so many helps to living as we ought, and doing good in our Generation: In short, to be always Happy, while we possess our Minds, with a good conscience, are free from the slavery of vices, and conform our Actions and Conversation to the Rules of right Reason. (*Works*, 4:55-56)

No one (except a contemporary ironic reader who notices that Dryden says nothing of the effects of Original Sin and "as a Christian surely . . .") who has read Renaissance and neoclassical moralsts expatiating on a piece of neo-Stoic doctrine is likely to doubt that Dryden is quite serious in his praise of Persius' philosophy. A passage from the third satire, in which a Stoic tutor admonishes his dissipated and idle pupil—still snoring away at eleven in the morning—and tells him that virtue is the most precious possession of all, was a favorite.

magne pater divum, saevos punire tyrannos
haud alia ratione velis, cum dira libido

moverit ingenium ferventi tincta veneno:
virtutem videant intabescantque relicta.
anne magis Siculi gemuerunt aera iuvenci,
et magis auratis pendens laquearibus ensis
purpureas subter cervices terruit, "imus,
imus praecipites" quam si sibi dicat et intus
palleat infelix, quod proxima nesciat uxor?　　　　　　[35-43]

[O great father of the gods, wish no other way to punish savage tyrants,
than that when a terrible desire soaked in burning venom has seized their
minds, they might see Virtue, and pine away from losing her. Did the
bronze of the Sicilian bull ever groan louder, or was the sword hanging
from the gilded ceiling ever more terrifying to the purple robed necks
beneath, than when one says to oneself, "you're slipping further and
further down," as the wretch turns pale within from a fear which his
wife beside him does not know about].⁶

The tutor (apparently rich Romans kept philosophers around
somewhat as noblemen in Dryden's time had chaplains) has added
a nice touch, that the worst punishment the vicious suffer is to
appreciate the beauty of goodness too late. (The early Christians
were to add a further turn of the knife, making the damned suffer
most by being given the briefest glimpse of the beatific vision; as
the poet William Empson put it, "This last pain for the damned
the Fathers found: / 'They knew the bliss with which they were
not crowned.' ")⁷ Dryden translates the passage even more freely
than usual.

　　Great Father of the Gods, when, for our Crimes,
Thou send'st some heavy Judgment on the Times;
Some Tyrant-King, the Terrour of his Age,
The Type, and true Vicegerent of thy Rage;
Thus punish him: Set Virtue in his Sight,
With all her Charms adorn'd; with all her Graces bright:
But set her distant; make him pale to see
His Gains out-weigh'd by lost Felicity!
　　Sicilian Tortures, and the Brazen Bull,
Are Emblems, rather than express the Full
Of what he feels: Yet what he fears, is more:

> The Wretch, who sitting at his plenteous Board,
> Look'd up, and view'd on high the pointed Sword
> Hang o'er his Head, and hanging by a Twine,
> Did with less Dread, and more securely Dine.
> Ev'n in his Sleep he starts, and fears the Knife;
> And, trembling, in his Arms, takes his Accomplice Wife:
> Down, down he goes, and from his Darling-Friend
> Conceals the Woes his guilty Dreams portend.   [65-83]

Dryden may have had in mind a plan more specific than giving Persius a Christian coloring. Notice how Persius' plural "saevos . . . tyrannos" has been changed to the singular and elevated to the royal throne—"Some Tyrant-King, the Terrour of his Age." It is also interesting that without any hint from Persius Dryden makes the wife not only lie beside ("proxima") her husband, but be his partner in crime ("Accomplice") as well. Considering that Dryden was a Roman Catholic, who lost his office of Poet Laureate at the fall of James II, we would probably not be indulging in wild speculation to see an allusion here to William of Orange and his consort Queen Mary. Dryden gives his tyrant-king a supernatural sanction by making him the "Type" of the divine "Rage," and because seventeenth-century readers found more allusions to Nero in Persius than modern commentators do, perhaps Dryden meant for us to associate William of Orange with Nero, who indeed had a "dira libido," and with the Beast of the book of Revelation.

Persius seems to have made Dryden uncomfortable. (I find him most at home with Ovid.)[8] Dryden likes broad ridicule, expansive couplet development, and a fancy on a very free rein. He is always ready to leap from translating his author to make any satirical point that crosses his mind (as in the case of William III). Perhaps he should not have attempted Persius, but editions of Juvenal traditionally included Persius, and Dryden's publisher Jacob Tonson, who always wanted more of Dryden's poetry than he could get, probably worried that readers would feel shortchanged without both satirists.

At least Dryden had some assistance on Persius. He noted that the first half of the second satire was translated "by one of my Sons, now in *Italy;* but I thought so well of it, that I let it pass without any Alteration" (*Works*, 4:291). As all three of Dryden's sons were in Italy at the time, we cannot tell which one composed some of the finest couplets in the entire volume. Persius had dedicated the poem to his friend Macrinus as a birthday present (obviously Persius believed in giving his friends something practical). It begins:

Hunc, Macrine, diem numera meliore lapillo,
qui tibi labentes apponit candidus annos.
funde merum genio. . . .

[Mark this day, Macrinus, with the better stone, the white one that reckons the years gliding by. Pour out wine to your genius.]⁹

The young Dryden translated the opening:

Let this auspicious Morning be exprest
With a white Stone, distinguished from the rest:
White as thy Fame, and as thy Honour clear;
And let new Joys attend, on thy new added year.
Indulge thy Genius, and o'reflow thy Soul,
Till thy Wit sparkle, like the chearful Bowl.

The enjambed opening line, the period extending through two couplets, and the chiasmus in the third line must have made the mature Dryden beam with paternal pride. (The last couplet may have appealed to Alexander Pope, who has a close parallel in his *Imitation of the First Satire of the Second Book of Horace*, 127-28.)

[III]

In the case of the satires of Juvenal that Dryden farmed out to other translators, we do not know what he let "pass without any Alteration." Fortunately, George Stepney's draft version of Juvenal's eighth satire survives in a manuscript that gives us some idea of the improvements Dryden may have suggested. Where Juvenal warns his idle aristocrat:

                                                              . . . at tu
nil nisi Cecropides truncoque simillimus Hermae.
nullo quippe alio vincis discrimine quam quod
illi marmoreum caput est, tua vivit imago.   [52–55]

[But you, if nothing but the descendant of the Founding Father, are just
like a limbless Herm. Indeed, you surpass it in no other way than that
it has a head of stone and you're a living statue.]

The manuscript version reads:

While You, Rubellius, who can barely boast
Your Birth from Cecrops, are so like the Post
which represents a Mercury, that this
betwixt both Blocks the onely diff'rence is,
why his to Yours should the precedence give,
His is a Marble-head, but thine doth live.   [90–95][10]

In the published translation we find instead:

While you, *Rubellius*, on your Birth relye;
Tho you resemble your Great Family
No more, than those rough Statues on the Road
(Which we call *Mercuries*) are like that God:
Your *Blockhead* tho excels in this alone,
You are a *Living Statue*, that of *Stone*.   [89–94]

Not only are the verses more sharply formed, but the reviser has
also eliminated the puzzling allusion to Cecrops (the legendary
founder of Athens). He has not been completely successful in
coping with foreign idioms and customs. Juvenal scornfully
compares the parasitic aristocrat to a monument with the head of
Hermes atop a solid block of stone. These "Herms" had no arms
or legs, but were fitted out with enormous genitals. "Useless as a
Herm" was a common expression. Dryden, if he was the reviser,
clarifies the comparison of the nobleman to a statue by adding a
new joke at his expense, telling him that he is as much like his
famous ancestors as a Herm is like the light and agile Hermes.

Whatever Dryden did for Stepney, I doubt very much that he made extensive changes in the work of most of his other collaborators. Their methods resemble Dryden's, though their couplets are cruder.[11] (Except, as we shall see, in the case of Thomas Creech.) There is no need to go over the work of each. One is curious to see, though, how they dealt with the less-esteemed satires, which contain explicit descriptions of sodomy and cannibalism. These were the second satire, the ninth satire—the sexually explicit interview with the male prostitute Naevolus—and the fifteenth satire, on the disgusting practices of the Egyptians. (Juvenal was not what we would call a "cultural relativist.")

The second satire was entrusted to Dryden's experienced lieutenant, who had written most of *The Second Part of Absalom and Achitophel*, Nahum Tate, now notorious for daring to rewrite *King Lear* with a happy ending to appeal to the tastes of Restoration audiences who wanted to see "poetic justice" done the innocent Cordelia. (Tate's *Lear* is in fact a much better play than we would infer from its reputation, derived mostly from Victorian "bardolators.") But Tate also possessed a keen sense of humor and had fun emphasizing the incongruity between the tough and virile outer appearance of the hairy Stoic men, and the smooth reality behind (quite literally) their facade. "Nulla fronti fides," says Juvenal in the famous tag—"don't trust appearances."

> . . . castigas turpia, cum sis
> inter Socraticos notissima fossa cinaedos?
> hispida membra quidem et durae per bracchia saetae
> promittunt atrocem animum, sed podice levi
> caeduntur tumidae medico ridente mariscae.   [9-13]

[Do you censure shameful deeds, while you're the best-known crevice among the Socratic queers? Hairy legs, indeed, and rough bristles on the arms proclaim an ascetic disposition, but swelling piles are sliced from your smooth buttocks by the laughing doctor.]

Like Dryden, Tate was not afraid to abandon the literal sense to capture Juvenal's spirit. (To see the difference, compare John Biddle's version of the same passage, in the chapter on Chapman and Biddle.)

Precise their Look, but to the Brothel come,
You'll know the Price of Philosophick Bum.
You'd swear, if you their Bristled Hides survey'd,
That for a Bear's Caresses they are made;
Yet of their Obscene Part they take such care,
That (like Baboons) they still keep *Podex* bare;
To see't so sleek and trimm'd the Surgeon smiles,
And scarcely can for laughing launce the Piles.   [13-20]

Tate clearly had some trouble with his verse. The "Brothel" is
here not because Juvenal (or Tate, for that matter) wanted to
suggest that the hypocritical moralist was a prostitute, but because
Tate needed a stressed and unstressed syllable so that he could end
the line with "come" and rhyme with "Bum" (a rhyme stolen
perhaps from one of the most delightful couplets in *MacFlecknoe*
— "From dusty Shops neglected Authors come, / Martyrs of Pies,
and Reliques of the Bum" [100-1]). Given Juvenal's fondness for
animal imagery, Tate did well to add the bear (had Dryden revised
the passage, though, surely he would have contrived to use it for
a triplet). When one reflects on how the fake philosopher con-
tracted piles and on the livid hue characteristic of the backside of
a baboon, it is easy too see why the surgeon could not keep from
laughing.

Dryden seems to have found Tate serviceable where delicacy
of sentiment and versification were less in demand than a strong
stomach, and assigned him the fifteenth satire, on Egyptian
cannibals. In it Juvenal described a battle between the men of two
Egyptian towns, Ombis and Tentyra. As the Ombites break ranks
and flee, one unfortunate slips and falls.

labitur hic quidam nimia formidine cursum
praecipitans capiturque. ast illum in plurima sectum
frustra et particulas, ut multis mortuus unus
sufficeret, totum corrosis ossibus edit
victrix turba, nec ardenti decoxit aeno
et veribus, longum usque adeo tardumque putavit
expectare focos, contenta cadavere crudo.
hic gaudere libet quod non violaverit ignem,

quem summa caeli raptum de parte Prometheus
donavit terris; elemento gratulor, et te
exultare reor. sed qui mordere cadaver
sustinuit, nil umquam hac carne libentius edit;
nam scelere in tanto ne quaeras et dubites an
prima voluptatem gula senserit; ultimus autem
qui stetit, absumpto iam toto corpore ductis
per terram digitis aliquid de sanguine gustat.   [77-92]

[Here one in headlong flight slips and is captured. After cutting him into bits and pieces, so that one dead man suffices for many, the victorious throng eat him down to the gnawed bones; neither did they cook him in a blazing kettle or on spits; they thought it would take too long to wait for a fire, and were content with a raw corpse. We should be pleased that they did not profane fire, which Prometheus stole from the very heights of heaven and gave to the earth; I congratulate the element and I think you'll be delighted too. But he who chewed the corpse never ate such meat more heartily in his life, in case you're wondering if only the first man in line enjoyed this pleasure—after the entire body had been consumed, the one who stood last in line tasted some of the blood by drawing his fingers through the sand.]

Typically, Juvenal organized the passage in a three part structure building toward a climax. First Juvenal tells us how the crowd hacked the victim into pieces, then, seeming to mitigate the offense, points out that at least they did not cook him, but this culinary omission adds to the atrocity—the crowd simply could not wait for the corpse to cook before they ate it. Then Juvenal interupts with one of his mock-epic apostrophes to congratulate Promethean fire for escaping pollution from human flesh. Most satirists would have stopped there. (Here I sympathize with critics who feel that no moralist ever would have begun the fifteenth satire in the the first place.) But Juvenal has more to add. Everyone ate with relish; he goes on to tell us. Even the unfortunate wretch who missed the main course of the banquet was delighted that he could at least lick the blood from the dust.

Unlike the master, Dryden, Tate had trouble joining his couplets into larger units to move towards a climax. Four lines approach his limit. But he has Dryden's weakness for triplets. And though he cannot catch Juvenal's tone of horrified, but fascinated, disgust, Tate sounds both jolly and contemptuous, as if he were telling one of those jokes about cannibals and missionaries.

An *Ombite* Wretch (by head-long hast betray'd,
And falling down i'th' Rout) is Pris'ner made.
Whose Flesh, torn off by Lumps, the Rav'nous Foe
In Morsells cut, to make it further go.
His Bones clean Pickt, his very Bones they gnaw;
No Stomack's baulkt because the Corpse is raw.
T' had been lost Time to Dress him—keen Desire
Supplies the want of Kettle, Spit, and Fire.
(*Prometheus* Ghost is sure o're-joy'd to see
His Heav'n-stol'n Fire from such disaster free.
Nor seems the sparkling Element less pleas'd than he).
The Guests are found too num'rous for the Treat,
But all, it seems, who had the Luck to Eat,
Swear they ne're tasted more Delicious Meat.
They swear, and such good Palates you shou'd trust,
Who doubts the Relish of the first free gust?
Since one who had i'th' Rear excluded been,
And cou'd not for a Taste o'th' Flesh come in,
Licks the soild Earth, which he thinks full as good;
While reeking with a mangled *Ombit*'s Blood.   [102-21]

I think Juvenal would have approved of calling the diners "Guests" and the main course a "Treat."

The second and fifteenth satires seem a comparatively easy assignment when one thinks of having to translate the infamous ninth satire, in which the male hustler Naevolus tells exactly how he goes about making his living in a passage which some Renaissance humanists who admired Juvenal's satire believed excluded him from the ranks of acceptable authors.[12] Naevolus is complaining to Juvenal about the meanness of his patron Virro:

. . . numera sestertia quinque
omnibus in rebus, numerentur deinde labores.

an facile et pronum est agere intra viscera penem
legitimum atque illic hesternae occurrere cenae?
servus erit minus ille miser qui foderit agrum,
quam dominum. . . .   [41–46]

[Count five thousand sesterces in exchange for all these services; that's
how my labors are rewarded. As if it were easy to drive an erect prick
far enough into him to come all over yesterday's dinner. The slave who
plows the master's field is less miserable than the slave who plows the
master.]

Stephen Harvey (spelled "Hervey" in the original edition), who
undertook this satire for Dryden, is wordier than Juvenal, but
unlike Victorian and even later translators leaves us in little doubt
about how Naevolus was expected to perform.

"Poor five *Sestertia* have been all my Gains,
And what is that for such detested Pains?
Was it an Ease and Pleasure, cou'd'st thou say
(Where Nature's Laws forbid) to force my way
To the digested Meals of yesterday?
The Slave more toil'd and harrass'd will be found,
Who Digs his Master's Buttocks, than his Ground."   [87–93]

I doubt Harvey received much help from Dryden here. The odd
contrast between the gross content of line 91 and its jaunty
rhythm, the awkward pyrrhus in the fourth foot in line 93, and
the "low words" to eke out the line and set up the rhyme ("cou'd'st
thou say?" "will be found"), were probably inspired by Harvey's
own genius.

[IV]

One of Dryden's henchmen was judged by Samuel Johnson to
have surpassed even the master as being the only one of the "band"
to attend to Juvenal's "declamatory grandeur" and to try to find
an English equivalent—Thomas Creech.[13] Creech deserves a better reputation. His translation of Lucretius was to remain standard

throughout the eighteenth century, alongside Dryden's Virgil and Pope's Homer. Scholars are perhaps repelled by his unfortunate version of Horace.[14] No one less like Horace can be easily imagined. But in 1684, when Creech's *The Odes, Satyres and Epistles of Horace* appeared, its publisher Tonson was trying to create a boom in translations and must have been happy to find a classical scholar who could turn out competent verse. The book is dedicated to the star translator in Tonson's stable, Dryden himself.

The preface shows Creech reacting to the developments in translation during the 1670s and 1680s noted in the preceeding chapters, and moving away from the Imitation towards a more literal style.

Some few advis'd me to turn the *Satyres* to our own Times, they said that *Rome* was now rivall'd in her Vices, and Parallels for Hypocrisie, Profaneness, Avarice and the like were easie to be found: But those Crimes are so far out of my acquaintance, and since the Character is the same whoever the Person is, I am not so fond of being hated as to make any disobliging applications: Such pains would look like an impertinent labor to find a dunghill, only that I might satisfy an accountable humor of dirting one Man's Face, and bespattering another: Some have taken this way, and the ill-Nature of the World hath conspir'd to think their rudeness Wit; All their smartness proceeds from a sharp Humor in their Body, which falls into their Pen, and if it drops upon a Man's Reputation that is as bright and solid as polisht Steel, it sullys it presently, and eats thro. Such are never lov'd, or prais'd, but shun'd and fear'd, like Mad-Dogs, for their Teeth and Foam; and are excellently represented by *Lucan*'s Basilisk,

Who drives all other Serpents from the Plains,
And all alone in the vast Desart reigns. [A7r–A7v]

Here Creech is probably thinking of Rochester's attack on Dryden in the "Allusion to Horace."

As Creech was an accomplished couplet poet, it is odd that his Horace should be so stale and tepid. He might have done better to modernize, for as we have seen, Horace's vigor and colloquial

immediacy do not come through well in literal translation, especially when the translator is something of a prude.

Creech's version of a passage in the seventh satire of the second
book shows both the strengths and the weaknesses of Creech's
technique. This satire is a dialogue between Horace and his slave
Davus, which takes place during the Saturnalia, when slaves were
free to talk back to and to criticize their masters. Davus, we find,
has been talking to the doorkeeper of a Stoic philosopher, and has,
so to speak, been "born again." Full of zeal to be a witness for his
new faith, Davus sets out to raise Horace's consciousness by
instructing him in the Stoic paradox that only the *sapiens*—the
wise man—is truly free. The rest of us, of whatever social position
or occupation, are actually slaves in thrall to our passions. To
prove that Horace is really the more abject slave, Davus ticks off
his master's dominant passions and naturally soon arrives at lust.

"te conjunx aliena capit, meretricula Davum:
peccat uter nostrum cruce dignius? acris ubi me
natura intendit, sub clara nuda lucerna
quaecumque excepit turgentis verbera caudae
clunibus aut agitavit equum lascivia supinum,
dimittit neque famosum neque sollicitum ne
ditior aut formae melioris meiat eodem.
tu cum proiectis insignibus, anulo equestri
Romano habitu, prodis ex iudice Dama,
turpis odoratum caput obscurante lacerna,
non es quod similas? metuens induceris atque
altercante libidinibus tremis ossa pavore.
quid refert, uri virgis ferroque necari
auctoratus eas, an turpi clausus in arca,
quo te demisit peccati conscia erilis,
contractum genibus tangas caput? estne marito
matrone peccantis in ambo iusta potestas,
in corruptorem vel iustior? illa tamen se
non habitu mutatve loco peccatve superne,
cum te formidet mulier neque credat amanti.
ibis sub furcam prudens, dominoque furenti
conmittes rem omnem et vitam et cum corpore famam
evasti. . . ."   [46-68]

["Someone else's wife takes your fancy, a little whore takes Davus'. Which of us commits the sin more deserving crucifixion? When fierce desire urges me on, whatever woman, nude in the clear lamplight, receives the battering of my swollen prick, or wantonly bounces her bottom on top of me as if I were a horse, won't send me away without my reputation or afraid that some fellow who's richer or handsomer will take my place. You, after putting aside your badges of rank, your knight's ring, and the dress of a Roman citizen, look like a shameful slave instead, and when you've covered your well-oiled head with a cloak, aren't you exactly what you seem to be? Although you're afraid you press on as your bones tremble with opposing waves of lust and fear. Does it matter whether you get whipped with rods or killed with steel or sold as a gladiator, or are hidden in some filthy trunk, in which the maid, who knows all about her mistress's sins, has shut you up with your head touching your knees? Isn't there just authority (that is, the husband's) over both (the wife and her lover) when the wife sins? Indeed, his authority over a seducer is more just. Yet she does not have to disguise herself or leave the house or be the principal sinner, since as a woman she was afraid that you would betray her. You go under the fork (that is, into enslavement) and trust a jealous husband with everything you own and your life and your reputation along with your body itself."]

It would be too much to expect Creech could reproduce Davus' coarse descriptions of just what he likes his "meretricula"— another satiric diminuitive that does not translate—to do for him, as well as the pleasure he takes in imagining his master in disguise slinking off to an assignation hot with desire but terrified of getting caught and in detailing all the horrible things that will happen to Horace if he is caught flagrante delicto; the very best he can hope for is that the maid will find him a trunk to hide in.

> You love Mens Wives, and I, my little Whores,
> Which is the greatest Fault now, mine or yours?
> When Nature Fires, and they have quencht my flame,
> I'm satisfi'd, nor do I loose my Fame,
> Nor fear that they will Jilt, and entertain
> A wittier, richer, and a finer Man.
> But when you slily sneak abroad by night,
> Your Rings and all the Habit of a Knight,

Thy *Roman* garb thrown off; from nobly brave
You sink into the Figure of a Slave:
A nasty Vail thrown o're thy fragrant Head,
And softly brought to an Adulterous Bed
Are you not such a One as you appear?
When introduc't you shake and tremble there,
Thy raging Lust disputing with thy Fear:
What difference is it whether you engage
To fight for hire, and bear the Victor's rage,
Be cut and slash't and kill'd upon the Stage?
Or by the Conscious Chamber-Maid be prest
Quite double, neck and heels into a Chest?
Hath not the injur'd Husband of the Whore
To punish both a right and Lawful Power?
And will not all his fiercest rage be just
On thee, that didst debauch her to thy Lust?
Yet she ne're changes Garb, nor shifts her place,
Nor takes such pains to get the foul embrace;
Nor injures Heaven, nor swears such Oaths as you,
Whilst the fond Creature doubts you'll prove untrue.
But wise you venture Slaves severest Fate
And to a man enrag'd, and swoln with hate,
Commit thy Fame, thy Life, and thy Estate.   [66–96]

   Even in the case of the pedestrian style of Horace, we have seen
that the slipshod splayfooted couplets of old-fashioned *satyr* were
an inadequate medium for the translator. Here I think that Creech
went too far in the opposite direction. The diction and versification are too elevated for the context. One could not expect Creech's
Davus to be as explicit as Horace's in discussing his sexual
preferences, but "When Nature Fires, and they have quencht my
flame" sounds like Lord Rochester in one of his more delicate
moments, not an English servant speaking to his master. Of
course, Creech may be trying to give us a Davus aping the
language of the upper classes, but if so he ought to have provided
some clues through malapropisms or mispronunciations (as, for
example, in nineteenth-century novels when servants mistakenly
asperate words beginning with vowels, as in "hable" and "hape,"

to avoid "dropping their aitches"). The couplets are also too well constructed for the *sermo pedestris*. Notice Creech's fondness of the medial caesura, and for clear, emphatic, and usually monosyllabic rhymes, and for tricolonic arrangements ("Be cut and slash't and kill'd"; "thy fame, thy life, and thy estate"), all of which remind us that Davus is using poetry, not everyday speech.

Philosophic poetry was another matter for Creech, and Dryden did well to pick him to render Juvenal's thirteenth satire, whose rhetorical effects and glittering *sententiae* need no flair for disguising verse as common conversation, but rather facility for balanced and steady, if somewhat stiff and predictable, couplets. Creech's translation even looks different on the page from the rest. Unlike any of the other satires in the volume, the thirteenth is broken into twenty-three sections, each designated by a roman numeral between the lines in the body of the text. These correspond to an outline of the contents given before the translation begins. (Each of the satires preceeded by a precis, but none of the others is quite as elaborate.) At a glance it looks as if Creech were emulating Wetenhall and attempting to turn the tenth satire into a Pindaric ode. In fact the couplets are in standard iambic pentameter.

The passage on atheists and optimists shows masterful technique. The soaring rate of fraud, embezzlement, and perjury, says Juvenal, is the work of two different kinds of criminals. First there are atheists, who do not have to worry about being punished by offended—but fortunately nonexistent—deities. There are also believers, who know that there are gods who punish sinners, but who think the punishment worth the crime, and who hope that the gods will take their time in getting round to inflicting it. They may not even bother at all.

> sunt in fortunae qui casibus omnia ponant
> et nullo credant mundum rectore moveri
> natura volvente vices et lucis et anni,
> atque ideo intrepidi quaecumque altaria tangunt.
> est alius metuens ne crimen poena sequatur,
> hic putat esse deos et peierat, atque ita secum;
> "decernat quodcumque volet de corpore nostro

Isis et irato feriat mea lumina sistro,
dummodo vel caecus teneam quos abnego nummos.
et phthisis et vomicae putres et dimidium crus
sunt tanti. pauper locupletem optare podagram
nec dubitet Ladas, si non eget Anticyra nec
Archigene; quid enim velocis gloria plantae
praestat et esuriens Pisaeae ramus olivae?
ut sit magna, tamen certe lenta ira deorum est;
si curant igitur cunctos punire nocentes,
quando ad me venient? sed et exorabile numen
fortasse experiar, solet his ignoscere. multi
committunt eadem diverso crimina fato:
ille crucem sceleris pretium tulit, hic diadema." [86-105]

[Some think all things are the result of chance, and they believe that the sky revolves with no governor to move it, but that nature controls the succession of days and years. So they will swear fearlessly on any altar at all. There is another sort who fears lest punishment follow the crime. He believes that there are gods, but commits perjury anyway, saying to himself: "Let Isis do anything she wants to my body and strike me blind with her angry sistrum, as long as that even as a blind man I can keep the money I refused to return. It is worth lung disease and disgusting ulcers and a broken leg. If Lada (a famous runner) were poor he would not hesitate to have the chance to suffer the rich man's gout if he did not need hellebore or the good offices of Archigenes (that is, as long as he was in his right mind). What does the glory of a fast foot and the branch of a Pisaen olive do for you if you are hungry? And though it may be great indeed, surely the wrath of the gods is slow. If indeed they bother to punish all of the wicked, when will they ever get to me? And perhaps I'll find the godhead merciful, with a forgiving nature. Many commit the same crime with different results—one gets crucified, another crowned."]

As the divisions show, Creech saw that while Juvenal speaks of only two classes of malefactors, his arrangement is tripartite.

X

Some think that *Chance* rules all, that *Nature* steers
The moving Seasons, and turns round the Years.
These run to every Shrine, These boldly swear,

And keep not *Faith*, because they know no *Fear*.

XI

Another doubts, but as his Doubts decline,
He dreads just Vengeance, and he starts at Sin;
He owns a *God:* and yet the Wretch forswears;
And thus he Reasons to relieve his Fears.
Let *Isis* Rage, so I securely hold
The Coin forsworn, and keep the ravisht Gold;
Let Blindness, Lameness come; are Legs and Eyes
Of *equal* Value to so great a Prize?
Would starving *Ladas,* had he leave to chuse,
And were not frantick, the *Rich Gout* refuse?
For can the Glory of the swiftest pace
Procure his Food? Or can he Feast on Praise?

XII

The Gods take *Aim* before they strike their blow,
Tho' *sure* their Vengeance, yet the Stroak is *slow;*
And shou'd at *evry* Sin their Thunder fly,
I'm yet secure, nor is my Danger nigh:
But they are *Gracious,* but their Hands are free,
And who can tell but they may reach to *Me?*
Some they forgive, and every Age relates
That *equal* Crimes have met *unequal* Fates;
That Sins *alike, unlike* Rewards have found,
And whilst *This* Villain's Crucifi'd, *The other*'s Crown'd. [110-35]

No other translator, not even Dryden himself, tries so hard make the couplets reproduce the stately movement of the dactylic hexameters as they unroll a series of rhetorical questions setting up the antithesis—"ille crucem . . . hic diadema" at the beginning and end of the final verse. Creech exhibits a masterful display of couplet structures and arrangements that prefigures the technique of Alexander Pope (whose debts to Creech's Lucretius have not been fully evaluated).[15] He uses words of like ending (*homoteleuton*) but opposite meaning in parallel ("*equal* Crimes . . . *unequal* Fates") and also chiastic ("Sins *alike, unlike* Rewards") orders, and as in the translation of Horace the rhymes are ringing and strong and the couplets well-balanced. Creech knows how to create irony through alliteration of similar sounds: "And keep not *Faith*, because they know no *Fear*" (notice how the alliteration occurs at the end of each half-line); "tho' *sure* their Vengeance, yet the Stroak is *slow*" (chiastic order here); and best of all, "And whilst *This* Villain's Crucifi'd, *The other*'s Crown'd." It is appropriate that the unfortunate Creech's version of the thirteeth satire was singled out by Dr. Johnson for special commendation, for Creech's versification and diction remind one remarkably of Johnson's in *The Vanity of Human Wishes*.

Notes

Preface

1 For Horace I used especially *Horace's Satires and Epistles*, trans. Jacob Fuchs (New York: Norton, 1977); and *Horace: The Satires*, ed. Edward P. Morris (New York, 1939; rpt. Norman: Univ. of Oklahoma Press, [1968]). For Juvenal, *The Satires of Juvenal*, trans. Rolfe Humphries (Bloomington: Indiana Univ. Press, 1958); *Juvenal*, ed. Henry Parks Wright (Boston: Ginn, 1901); *D. Iunii Iuuenalis Saturae XIV*, ed. J. D. Duff, with a new introduction by Michael Coffey (Cambridge: Cambridge Univ. Press, 1970); and E. Courtney, *A Commentary on the Satires of Juvenal* (London: Athlone Press, 1980). For Persius, *The Satires of Persius*, trans. W. S. Merwin (Bloomington: Indiana Univ. Press, 1961); and *The Satires of A. Persius Flaccus*, ed. Basil L. Gildersleeve (New York, 1875; rpt. New York: Arno Press, 1979).

2 A pioneering study of this problem was J. McG. Bottkol's "Dryden's Latin Scholarship," *Modern Philology* 40 (1943): 241-54.

3 The basic text for Horace was *Q. Horati Flacci Opera*, ed. Fridericus Klingner, 3d. ed. (Leipzig: Teubner, 1959); for Persius, Gildersleeve's edition, the text of which is essentially that of Otto Jahn's 1868 Leipzig edition, and for Juvenal *D. Iunius Juvenalis: Saturae mit kritischem Apparat*, ed. Ulrich Knoche (Munich: Max Hueber, 1950). Brackets indicating suspected interpolations have been ignored, punctuation and capitalization sometimes altered, and quotation marks made to follow current American practice.

4 For convenience, Holyday's Persius is quoted from the 1673 translation of Juvenal and Persius, not the 1616 Persius. The three editions of Stapleton's Juvenal containing substantive changes are all

quoted. The absence of the long-awaited edition of John Oldham by Harold F. Brooks is lamentable.

Ben Jonson, Juvenal, and Horace

1 See David McPherson, "Ben Jonson's Library and Marginalia: An Annotated Catalogue," *Studies in Philology* 71, no. 5 (1974): 56; and Kathryn A. McEuen, "Jonson and Juvenal," *Review of English Studies* 21 (1944): 92-103.

2 H. A. Mason, "Is Juvenal a Classic?" [answer: no!] in *Critical Essays on Roman Literature: Satire*, ed. J. P. Sullivan (London: Routledge & Kegan Paul, 1963), p. 113.

3 As Jonson's editors have remarked. See C. H. Herford, Percy Simpson, and Evelyn Simpson, eds., *Ben Jonson*, 11 vols. (Oxford: Clarendon Press, 1925-52), 9:633-34.

4 See John G. Sweeney, III, "*Sejanus* and the People's Beastly Rage," *ELH* 48 (1981): 61-82.

5 Critics have disagreed whether Jonson made Truewit too contemptuous. See Jonas A. Barish, "Ovid, Juvenal, and *The Silent Woman*," *PMLA* 71 (1956): 213-24; and John Ferns, "Ovid, Juvenal, and 'The Silent Woman': A Reconsideration," *Modern Language Review* 65 (1970): 248-53.

6 We know Renaissance readers caught many of the allusions. See James A. Riddell, "Seventeenth-Century Identifications of Jonson's Sources in the Classics," *Renaissance Quarterly* 28 (1975): 204-18.

7 Thersites, in Shakespeare's *Troilus and Cressida*, is a good example of the breed. See Alvin Kernan, *The Cankered Muse: Satire of the English Renaissance* (New Haven: Yale Univ. Press, 1959).

8 For how low, see *Hamlet* 4.5.62-63.

9 In the *Epilogue to the Satires: Dialogue II*, the ironically named "Friend" advises Alexander Pope: "Spare then the Person, and expose the Vice." Pope replies, "How Sir! Not damn the Sharper, but the Dice?" Alexander Pope, *Imitations of Horace*, ed. John Butt, The Twickenham Edition of the Poems of Alexander Pope, 11 vols. (London: Methuen; New Haven: Yale Univ. Press, 1939-69), 4:314, ll. 12-13. Of course, there are always people who imagine themselves or their favorite causes the objects of satires whose authors never gave them a moment's thought.

10 An interesting exception is in the handling of chronology. Jonson not only makes Virgil and Ovid contemporaries, but even has Ovid's exile take place in the play. I expect that most Renaissance readers were not so much ignorant of chronology (after all, they had mostly the same texts we do) as indifferent to it.

11 The silliest was probably Edmund Wilson, who remarked: "Ben Jonson seems an obvious example of a psychological type which has been described by Freud and designated by a technical name, *anal erotic.*" *The Triple Thinkers: Twelve Essays on Literary Subjects* (New York: Oxford Univ. Press, 1948), p. 217.

Early Seventeenth-Century Translations

1 The attribution to William Barksted, an actor, minor dramatist, and poet, is not certain.

2 For Renaissance interpretations of Horace's dictum, see Glyn P. Norton, *"Fidus Interpres:* A Philological Contribution to the Philosophy of Translation in Renaissance France," in *Neo-Latin and Vernacular in Renaissance France,* ed. Grahame Castor and Terence Cave (Oxford: Clarendon Press, 1984), pp. 227-51.

3 G. L. Brodersen, "Seventeenth-Century Translations of Juvenal," *Phoenix* 7 (1953): 64.

4 Too often followers of Ezra Pound's maxim "Make it new" demonstrate anew that novelty and good poetry are not always the same thing. When well done, as in Samuel Johnson's *The Vanity of Human Wishes,* wholesale recasting and modernization can be impressive. But, as in the case of Barksted, originality can make what would have been merely bad unendurable. Take what happens when Robert Bagg renders the opening words of Euripides' *Bacchae* (spelled, predictably, *Bakkhai* [Amherst: Univ. of Massachusetts Press, 1978]) as "I'm back!" Dionysus sounds as if he had just returned, not to ancient Thebes, but home from a twentieth-century American supermarket.

5 *The Shorter Poems of Sir John Beaumont: A Critical Edition with an Introduction and Commentary,* ed. Roger D. Sell, Acta Academiae Aboensis, ser. A Humaniora, 49 (Åbo [Turku, Finland]: Åbo Akademi, 1974), p. 87.

6 William Bowman Piper, *The Heroic Couplet* (Cleveland: Press of Case Western Reserve University, 1969), p. 232.

7 See *Poems of Sir John Beaumont*, ed. Sell, p. 9.

8 As in *Twelfth Night* 4.2.50-60.

9 The Romans' use of diminutives is difficult for the English translator. Except for *boy* and *girl* to refer informally to adult men and women ("boyfriend," "girl-talk"), English speakers generally use diminutives only when speaking to infants and pets. An English Catullus could hardly refer to his mistress's pet sparrow as a "poor little birdy" ("miselle passer") or to his mistress's eyes as "little eyeies" ("ocelli"), or to his friend's new girlfriend as a "little whorey" ("scortillum").

10 Not that he never does. As Sell remarks, in the translation of the tenth satire, Beaumont "on a much larger scale than in his other translations uses his own extra length to clarify points for the benefit of the contemporary English reader, whether by paraphrase, by generalization, or by using terms drawn from English, rather than Roman, culture and institutions." *Poems of Sir John Beaumont*, p. 317.

11 As William Anderson remarks, the dolls are symbols of the girls' virginity and so would be of little use to the goddess of love. *The Satires of Persius*, trans. W. S. Merwin, intro. and notes William S. Anderson (Bloomington: Indiana Univ. Press, 1961), p. 111.

12 It is important to clarify what one means by "elevated." In Juvenal's case, elevation and sublimity had nothing whatever to do with the qualities those words connoted to the Victorians. They refer purely to rhetorical and stylistic effects. See my note "Juvenal as Sublime Satirist," *PMLA* 89 (1972): 508-11, in response to W. B. Carnochan's "Satire, Sublimity, and Sentiment: Theory and Practice in Post-Augustan Satire," *PMLA* 85 (1970): 260-67. I think now that I may have overstated the continuity of Juvenal's reputation. But that is a story to be told in another place.

13 *Poems of Sir John Beaumont*, ed. Sell, p. 318. Compare Johnson's equivalent, in *The Vanity of Human Wishes*, of Beaumont's ll. 29-30: "Nor Light nor Darkness bring his Pain Relief, / One shews the Plunder, and one hides the Thief" [43-44]).

14 For the Latin original, see pp. 75-76.

Barton Holyday's Juvenal and Persius

1 *Decimus Junius Juvenalis, and Aulus Persius Flaccus Translated and Illustrated, As well with Sculpture as Notes* (Oxford, 1673).

2 Brodersen states, "the whole work, annotations and all, was probably complete at least by 1646." "Seventeenth-Century Translations of Juvenal," p. 69.

3 Anthony à Wood, *Athenae Oxonienses*, 2 vols. (London, 1691-92), 2:259.

4 *The Works of John Dryden*, 20 vols. planned, ed. H. T. Swedenberg, Jr., et al. (Berkeley and Los Angeles: Univ. of California Press, 1956-), 4:88-89. Hereafter cited as *Works*.

5 Loggan may have relied considerably on the last. There is an odd drawing of a beaver (illustrating Juvenal's satire 12, verse 34) with the body of a dog and teeth like a werewolf's. Even stranger are the only illustrations that I have ever seen of *fibulae* (on Juvenal's satire 6, verse 73—believing sex was bad for the voice, the Romans infibulated male singers). One of the devices Loggan depicts would certainly prevent intercourse by threatening any prospective partner with a grisly fate; I could not and do not want to figure out how the other would work. But I should like to know whether the lurid mind that conceived them belonged to Loggan, to some earlier illustrator, or to a maker of spurious antiquities whose clients had curious tastes.

6 What little is known of the festival is described in H. H. Scullard, *Festivals and Ceremonies of the Roman Republic* (London: Thames & Hudson, 1981), pp. 199-201. Scullard remarks that "it need not have degenerated under the Empire into the drunken orgy depicted by the moralist and satirist, Juvenal."

7 "Recalling our reconstruction of Juvenal's life, we might suggest that, after coming up to Rome from his country town, he had an unhappy experience with the proud and selfish Roman ladies. It looks as though, while waiting for the appointment in government service which never came, he married a lady of superior rank and pretensions, and found her intolerable." Gilbert Highet, *Juvenal the Satirist: A Study* (Oxford: Clarendon Press, 1954), p. 103. I think Juvenal was probably drawn to the subject because it offered him a chance to expatiate on his favorite theme, aristocratic misbehavior. As Scullard, *Festivals and Ceremonies*, remarks, "in the later Republic [and presumably in Juvenal's day too] only a limited number of socially acceptable women are likely to have been allowed to attend" (p. 200).

8 See H. H. Scullard, *The Elephant in the Greek and Roman World* (London: Thames and Hudson, 1974), pp. 198-200.

9 Although Holyday stayed with its "vulgar name" in his translation, his illustrations show that he knew that Diogenes' dwelling was not a wooden vessel for bathing or washing, but a *dolium*, a large wine jar made of clay. This couplet may sound funny to us because the only item one has "bespoke" these days is a Savile Row suit. But from the citations in the *Oxford English Dictionary*, it appears that even in the seventeenth century "bespoke" implied high-quality custom-made goods.

10 Gildersleeve, p. 121.

11 What, one wonders, are future translators of twentieth-century writers going to make of such terms as "class consciousness," "superego," and "patriarchy"?

12 *The Classical Papers of A. E. Housman*, 3 vols., ed. J. Diggle and F. R. D. Goodyear (Cambridge: Cambridge Univ. Press, 1972), 2:852.

13 Gildersleeve's 1875 commentary contains a delightful note: "All people of 'culture' talked about 'horoscope,' 'nativity,' and 'malign aspect,' just as the same class in our time speak of 'the spectroscope,' 'heat a mode of motion,' and 'the survival of the fittest' (p. 162)."

George Chapman's and John Biddle's Translations from Juvenal

1 Millar MacLure refers to it in "The Minor Translations of George Chapman," *Modern Philology* 60 (1963): 172-82. MacLure's "general impression is of a strong, roughly textured version, often inaccurate, oftener awkward, but occasionally firm and eloquent ... " (p. 181). My opinion is higher, probably because some early versions of Juvenal were a good deal rougher; by comparison Chapman seems smooth indeed.

2 MacLure notes, "which underscores the irony." "Minor Translations," p. 180.

3 Some comments can, or at least should, be made only in French. This is Alfred Ernout's on Petronius' similar reference to the wine served by Trimalchio labeled "Falernum Opimianum annorum centum." *Pétrone: Le Satiricon*, ed. and trans. Alfred Ernout (Paris: Société d'Edition "Les Belles Lettres," 1962), p. 20.

4 The ancients thought that good wine in moderate amounts alleviated gastritis. Duff's edition of Juvenal quotes Celsius (3:19), and Paul gave similar advice to Timothy (1 Tim. 5.24).

5 Folio A3v. MacLure suggests that Chapman's translations may have received "some pretty sharp remarks from Jonson" ("Minor Transla-

tions," p. 180), whose practice, as we have seen, was to remain closer to the vocabulary and style of the Latin.

6 *Iunii Iuuenalis et Auli Persii Flacci Satyrae: Cum annotationibus ad marginem quae obscurissima quaeque dilucidare possint*, ed. Thomas Farnaby (London, 1612), was reprinted in 1615, 1620-21, and 1633. Biddle's "That for a Supper hop't before they went" corresponds to Farnaby's gloss on verse 132, "Post longam coenae expectationem," "choicest Sea fish . . . choicest Ven'son" to the gloss on 135, "Optimas feras & delicatissmos pisces." On the other hand, "Smell-feast" again reminds one of Chapman, but the expression seems to have been common in the earlier seventeenth century.

7 Biddle's text reads *Teribonius*, but since the variant appears in no editon of Juvenal I could find, I think it is a typographical error.

8 The *Oxford English Dictionary* cites Sir John Harington's translation of Ariosto's *Orlando Furioso*, canto 7, stanza 62.

Juvenal and Horace in the Civil War and Interregnum

1 Brodersen has noticed that in dedication to the the 1660 version of Juvenal, Stapleton asserts that he began his translation in 1638. "Seventeenth-Century Translations of Juvenal," p. 68.

2 How much did Stapleton owe Holyday? In the dedication to Holyday's translation, Holyday's son-in-law William Dewey refers to the "light the other Translation already extant borrowed from this Taper," and in Stapleton's notes (but not, so far as I have been able to find, in the text), there are small but unmistakable traces of Stapleton's thefts. The note on Fronto (cf. Holyday's, discussed earlier in the third chapter) in the 1644 version reads: "*Julius Fronto*, a noble *Roman*, who in the heate of *August*, when the Poets used to read their workes, accommodated them with shady Walks and marble Galleries." That poets recited in August comes from the third satire, but the shady walks and the grounds open to poets recall Holyday. In one note Holyday clearly is irritated at Stapleton for garbling the information he provided. Early in the fourth satire Juvenal has an apostrophe to the wealthy reprobate Crispinus, whom Juvenal says seduced even one of the Vestal Virgins, who, if they were unchaste, were buried alive to expiate this sacrilege. As Stapleton describes the process in 1644: "A Vestall virgin, who upon proofe of a breach of her vow of Chastity was to be carried out of the *Colin* Gate to the *Campus Sceleratus*, or Field of execution,

and there in her close Chaire to be let down into a Vault, wherein was a Couch a Lampe burning, and a little meate. The hole they put her in at was presently stopped up, and so the poore *Anchorite* lived and died in her grave . . ." (p. 111). Holyday's note on the same passage reads: "At *Porta Collina* (on the North-East side of old *Rome*) within the City, as *Plutarch* describes it, in a roome under the ground there was prepar'd a Bed, a burning Light, and (as the cheif parts of food) a little bread, water and milk. The *Vestal* was bound alive and layd on a biere, and so carried through the *Forum* with great Silence and Horror. When they came to the cave, the biere being set down, *deposito feretro* (*not let down* into the vault) and she unbound, the Priest praying somewhat secretely, brought her and set her on a ladder, *by which she descended*, and presently turning back from her, the ladder being drawn up, they threw-in earth, and fill'd up the Cave's mouth" (p. 68). Stapleton must have misread a long *s* as an *l* and Holyday's italics show awareness of the bungled theft.

3 The artists were Robert Streater, John Danckerts, and Francis Barlow, the engraver was Wenceslaus Hollar. There was one illustration for each satire. They were copied for the second edition (1697) of Dryden's Juvenal, and some are reproduced in *Works*, vol. 4. But the 1660 originals are much clearer.

4 *The Complete Poetry of Henry Vaughan*, ed. French Fogle (New York: Doubleday, 1964), pp. 5-6. Italics reversed.

5 Alan Rudrum, *Henry Vaughan*, Writers of Wales ([Cardiff]: Univ. of Wales Press, 1981), p. 8, calls Vaughan's statement "a neatly delivered suggestion that his enemies were unlettered as well as rebellious."

6 F. E. Hutchinson, *Henry Vaughan: A Life and an Interpretation* (Oxford: Clarendon Press, 1947), pp. 41-43. Alan Rudrum, ed., *Henry Vaughan: The Complete Poems* (Harmondsworth, Middx.: Penguin Books, 1976; rpt. New Haven: Yale Univ. Press, 1981), p. 463, believes that lines 440-41, "Our publick vowes / Made *Caesar* guiltles; But sent him to loose / His head at Nile," are a reference to Charles's role in the condemnation of Strafford. But Juvenal here was referring to the assassination of Pompey, and if Strafford scarcely resembles Sejanus, even less was his situation like Pompey's.

7 Milton "was also able to elucidate a providential reason for the . . . fall of the Roman republic into the empire, a reason that acts as a kind of negative justification for the institution," according to Stevie Davies, who quotes Milton: "For stories teach us that libertie sought out of

season in a corrupt and degenerate age brought Rome it self into further slaverie. For libertie hath a sharp and double edge fitt onlie to be handl'd by just and vertuous men, to bad and dissolute it becomes a mischief unwieldie in thir own hands." *Complete Prose Works of John Milton,* vol. 5, *History of Britain and the Miltonic State Papers,* ed. French Fogel (New Haven: Yale U. Press, 1971), p. 449. "Under this perspective, Nero, Caligula, and Tiberius were conceived, delivered, and nourished by their own subjects," writes Davies in *Images of Kingship in* Paradise Lost: *Milton's Politics and Christian Liberty* (Columbia: Univ. of Missouri Press, 1983), p. 97.

8 Jonathan F. S. Post, *Henry Vaughan: The Unfolding Vision* (Princeton: Princeton Univ. Press, 1982), p. 22.

9 As Courtney remarks in his *Commentary on the Satires of Juvenal* on 354-55: "These lines include three diminutives and are clearly ironical in content. Juvenal suggests a lack of respect for the usual method of prayer with offerings and hints that prayer is an unnecessary concession to human weakness because we ourselves can provide its object (363). The irony however is hardly opportune here as it casts doubt on the sincerity of the following advice" (p. 486).

10 See Auden's delightful poem "The Horatians," in *Collected Poems,* ed. Edward Mendelson (London: Faber and Faber, 1976), pp. 579-81.

11 The fifth is quite nasty. It is spoken by a child Canidia is starving to death so she can use his liver in a love potion.

12 "Latin, an inflected language, makes possible effects that are impossible in our word-order English. Words not in agreement can be placed side by side for ironic effect; images can carry from one word to the next, the memory, the lingering overtone of the first making a chord, or a prism, with the second; the line, or the stanza, can be full of ambiguities or surprises, matters held in suspense, judgment on them changed as we go along, and the resolution not coming till the very end. Horace is the master of these effects, and the utter despair of all translators (except those who make him out a light-verse comic)." Rolfe Humphries, "Latin and English Verse—Some Practical Considerations," in *On Translation,* ed. Reuben Brower (Cambridge: Harvard Univ. Press, 1959), p. 61. Humphries was writing primarily of the odes, but Horace uses the same effects to a lesser extent in the satires.

13 For modern examples, compare Bovie's translation of the *Satires and Epistles of Horace* (Chicago: Univ. of Chicago Press, 1959) with

Humphries' *Satires of Juvenal*. Both seem to me quite successful, but Bovie has to use many more puns and anachronisms to get Horace's sly humor into English than Humphries needs for Juvenal's whopping hyperboles.

14 *Quinti Horatii Flacci Poemata, scholijs siue annotationibus, quae breuis commentarij vice esse possint à Ioanne Bond illustrata* (London, 1606), was reprinted in 1608, 1611, 1614, 1620, and 1630.

Early Restoration Adaptations

1 R. Selden, "Juvenal and Restoration Modes of Translation," *Modern Language Review* 68 (1973): 481-93. Because Selden confines himself to translations of Juvenal's tenth satire, he does not take into account the wide range from very literal translation to free Imitation in adaptations of the satires of Horace and of Juvenal's other satires.

2 For a useful treatment of Roman attitudes toward sex, love, and marriage, see chapter 1, "Traditional Attitudes to Love, the Moral and Social Background," in R. O. A. M. Lyne, *The Latin Love Poets from Catullus to Horace* (Oxford: Clarendon Press, 1980), pp. 1-18.

3 For the identities of the translators, see Harold F. Brooks, "Contributors to Brome's Horace," *Notes & Queries* 174 (1938): 200-01; and W. J. Cameron, "Brome's 'Horace' 1666 and 1671," *Notes & Queries* 202 (1957): 70-71.

4 As pointed out by Harold F. Brooks in "The 'Imitation' in English Poetry, Especially in Formal Verse Satire, before the Age of Pope," *Review of English Studies* 25 (1949): 124-40. Brooks's judgment was endorsed by Howard D. Weinbrot, *The Formal Strain: Studies in Augustan Imitation and Satire* (Chicago: Univ. of Chicago Press, 1969), p. 39.

5 Dustin H. Griffin, *Satires Against Man: The Poems of Rochester* (Berkeley and Los Angeles: Univ. of California Press, 1973), p. 249. Griffin cites Brooks but ignores Weinbrot's book.

6 *The Poems of John Wilmot, Earl of Rochester*, ed. David M. Vieth (New Haven: Yale Univ. Press, 1968), p. 249.

7 Vivian de Sola Pinto, in *Enthusiast in Wit: A Portrait of John Wilmot Earl of Rochester 1647-1680*, rev. ed. (London: Routledge & Kegan Paul, 1962), p. 98, has noticed the apparent reference to an earlier attack on Dryden. It may be, as Pinto suggests, that Rochester was simply

following Horace. But Horace really had discussed Lucilius in an earlier satire, and it is odd that in an Imitation Rochester would have felt bound by the example of his original to refer to a satire he had never written. Pat Rogers, "An Allusion to Horace," in *Spirit of Wit: Reconsiderations of Rochester*, ed. Jeremy Treglown (Oxford: Blackwell, 1982), p. 167, assumes that no such attack, at least in writing, occurred.

8 See the "Preface" to *All for Love* (1678), in *Four Tragedies*, ed. L. A. Beaurline and Fredson Bowers (Chicago: Univ. of Chicago Press, 1967), pp. 201-02. According to Frank Livingstone Huntley, "Dryden, Rochester, and the Eighth Satire of Juvenal," *Philological Quarterly* 18 (1939): 269-84, the "Preface to *All for Love* is a piece of epideictic rhetoric devoted to a censure of Rochester" (p. 284) based on the eighth satire of Juvenal.

9 Howard D. Weinbrot, in "The 'Allusion to Horace': Rochester's Imitative Mode," *Studies in Philology* 69 (1972): 348-68, remarks: "One of the central reasons why Rochester's poem is not fully satisfying is that the creative strengths of Imitation as a genre were not yet clear" (p. 368). David Farley-Hills notes: "[Rochester's] attempts to suggest Horatian standards for judgment are the least successful part of the poem. It is interesting that here at last he throws all his weight against the English Juvenalian tradition in favour of the Horatian. . . . Rochester's poetry thrives on the tension between the rebel and the reasonable man; here he is trying to insist on *noblesse oblige*, but the Satyr keeps revealing itself through the Horatian toga." *Rochester's Poetry* (London: Bell & Hyman, 1978), p. 203.

10 Text from *Poems on Affairs of State: Augustan Satirical Verse, 1660-1714*, 7 vols., ed. George deF. Lord, et al. (New Haven: Yale Univ. Press, 1963-75), 1:364. Hereafter cited as *POAS*.

11 See P. K. Elkin, *The Augustan Defence of Satire* (Oxford: Clarendon Press, 1974), pp.71-89.

12 See David M. Vieth, *Attribution in Restoration Poetry: A Study of Rochester's Poems of 1680* (New Haven: Yale Univ. Press, 1963), pp. 137-63, esp. p. 144. There are also accounts in Pinto, *Enthusiast in Wit*, pp. 162-63, and *POAS*, 1:366-67n.

13 *POAS*, 1:373.

The Imitation Is Perfected

1 James Sutherland, *English Literature of the Late Seventeenth Century*, Oxford History of English Literature (Oxford: Clarendon Press, 1969), p. 166.

2 Quoted from *Poems and Translations* (London, 1683), reprinted with *The Remains of Mr. John Oldham* (London, 1684).

3 Paul Hammond, *John Oldham and the Renewal of Classical Culture* (Cambridge: Cambridge Univ. Press, 1983), p. 120, believes the interest Oldham's bore shows in the price of hay owes something to the "Garrulous Man" in Theophrastus' *Characters*.

4 *POAS*, 2:425. For a full account of the affair, see B. J. Rahn, "*A Ra-ree Show*—A Rare Cartoon: Revolutionary Propaganda in the Treason Trial of Stephen College," in *Studies in Change and Revolution: Aspects of English Intellectual History 1640-1800*, ed. Paul J. Korshin (Menston, Yorks.: The Scolar Press, 1972), pp. 77-98.

5 See Harold F. Brooks, "John Oldham: Some Problems of Biography and Annotation," *Philological Quarterly* 54 (1975): 569-78. Brooks conjectures that the flier may actually have been named Aston or Tompion.

6 Hammond remarks, "Given Oldham's own social position, we may expect him to be deeply engaged when Juvenal writes about the plight of the poor. In particular we might look to the contrasting treatment meted out by society to the impoverished poet and the wealthy bachelor" and after Oldham's version of the passage, says, "Recalling Boileau [Satire 1], our first reaction may be to wonder at the restraint." *John Oldham*, p. 177.

7 Pordage is discussed by Christopher Hill in *The Experience of Defeat: Milton and Some Contemporaries* (New York: Viking, 1984), pp. 222-42.

8 Hammond, *John Oldham*, p. 180.

9 See Samuel Dill's engaging *Roman Society from Nero to Marcus Aurelius* (London: Macmillan, 1904), pp. 58-99; and also J. Wight Duff, *Roman Satire: Its Outlook on Social Life*, Sather Classical Lectures (Berkeley: Univ. of California Press, 1936), pp. 147-66.

10 Vieth, *Attribution in Restoration Poetry*, p. 437.

11 I mentioned the emendation to Professor Robert D. Hume, who

reminded me that as Oldham's *Works* were not published till 1684, it is possible that Wood never saw the name written down and concocted a phonetic spelling.

12 *The Works of Mr. John Oldham, together with His Remains* (London, 1684), pp. 84-86 [actually pp. 94-96]. The original has considerably more charm. But then they order this matter better in France.

Philis, cachez bien ses appas,
Les mortels ne dureroient pas,
Si ces beautez estoient sans voiles;
Les Dieux qui regnent dessus nous,
Assis là haut sur les Estoilles,
Ont un moins beau siege que vous.

Vincent Voiture, *Poésies*, 2 vols., ed Henri Lafay (Paris: Didier, 1971), 1:56.

Versions of the Late Eighties and Early Nineties

1 This splendid expression reminds one of the story about the Texan who tried to cook and eat an armadillo, and said, "The more I ate, the bigger that armadillo got."

2 For ironic readings of the thirteenth satire, see W. S. Anderson, "The Programs of Juvenal's Later Books," *Classical Philology* 57 (1962): 145-60, reprinted in his *Essays in Roman Satire* (Princeton: Princeton Univ. Press, 1982), pp. 277-92; A. D. Pryor, "Juvenal's False Consolation," *AULMA* 18 (1962): 167-80; Lowell Edmunds, "Juvenal's Thirteenth Satire," *Rheinisches Museum für Philologie* 115 (1972): 59-63; and Mark Morford, "Juvenal's Thirteenth Satire," *American Journal of Philology* 94 (1973): 26-36.

3 It would be interesting to know why Dryden provided a dedicatory poem for Higden's translation. At that time, Higden was suing Tonson, who had published the translation of the thirteenth satire, and who was also Dryden's publisher. Perhaps Dryden praised Higden only as a maneuver to get a better deal from Tonson. See C. E. Ward, "Some Notes on Dryden," *Review of English Studies* 13 (1937): 297-306.

4 See S. C. Fredericks, "Irony of Overstatement in the Satires of Juvenal," *Illinois Classical Studies* 4 (1979): 178-91.

5 See the editors' comments in *Works*, 3:325-26.

6 *The Complete Works of Thomas Shadwell*, 5 vols., ed. Montague Summers (London: Fortune Press, 1927), 5:294.

7 For such responses today see J. P. Sullivan, *Ezra Pound and Sextus Propertius: A Study in Creative Translation* (Austin: Univ. of Texas Press, 1964), who cites numerous examples from reviewers of Ezra Pound's *Homage to Sextus Propertius*.

8 In *Literary Works of Matthew Prior*, 2 vols., ed. H. Bunker Wright and Monroe K. Spears, 2d ed. (Oxford: Clarendon Press, 1971).

9 Harold F. Brooks, "Dryden's Juvenal and the Harveys," *Philological Quarterly* 48 (1969): 12-13.

10 Some modern scholars regard the tenth satire as a demonstration of the futility of prayer, a subject that probably arouses little enthusiasm from preachers. The traditional view still has adherents. Let me quote an eloquent one. "Juvenal's tenth satire was written by a poet who seems to have taken his role as a teacher of ethics seriously. In this satire he is above all concerned with the morality and well-being of the individual." Emin Tengström, *A Study of Juvenal's Tenth Satire: Some Structural and Interpretative Problems*, Studia graeca et latina Gothoburgensia 42 (Gothenburg: Acta Universitatis Gothoburgensis, 1980), p. 52.

11 Dennis's translation appeared in P. Motteaux, *The Gentleman's Journal; or the Monthly Miscellany* (London, 1692).

Dryden and His Myrmidons

1 Quoted from *Works*, 4:89.

2 Dryden's classic statement on the subject appeared in 1680, in his Preface to *Ovid's Epistles* (*Works*, 1:114-15): "All Translation I suppose may be reduced to these three heads:

"First, that of Metaphrase, or turning an Authour word by word, and Line by Line, from one Language into another. Thus, or near this manner, was *Horace* his Art of Poetry translated by *Ben. Johnson*. The second way is that of Paraphrase, or Translation with Latitude, where the Authour is kept in view by the Translator, so as never to be lost, but his words are not so strictly follow'd as his sense, and that too is admitted to be amplyfied, but not alter'd. Such is Mr. *Wallers* Translation of *Virgils* Fourth *Æneid*. The Third way is that of Imitation, where the Translator (if he has not lost that Name) assumes the liberty not only to vary from the words and sence, but to forsake them both as he sees occasion: and taking only some general hints from the Original, to run division on the ground-work, as he pleases. Such is Mr. *Cowleys* practice in turning two Odes of *Pindar*, and one of *Horace* into *English*."

Generically, Dryden's distinctions are unsatisfactory and I have made no use of them in this book, since adaptors so completely different as Barksted and Wetenhall would have to be lumped together with Rochester and Oldham as authors of Imitations. (Of course in 1680 Oldham's Imitations were unpublished and one can understand Dryden's ignoring Rochester's "Allusion.") Equally misleading too would be to call the translations by Beaumont, by Holyday, and by Stapleton, all metaphrases though they all stay close to the literal meaning of the original.

But if we take Dryden's terms as indicating methods of *translating*, rather than kinds of *translations*, then they can be used much more accurately to refer to what the poetic translator did. Thus we could say that Barksted begins with metaphrase, soon passes to paraphrase, and ends in the wildest form of Imitation. But I prefer the terms "close translation," "free translation," and "Imitation"—reserving the last for a substantially new poem built on a classical model—as more precise and and at the same time less technical.

3 The reason Marius drinks at the eighth hour, about two in the afternoon, is that the Romans did their drinking during and after dinner; they usually dined at the ninth hour, thus Marius was in a hurry for dinner.

4 These verses are quite difficult to understand and probably corrupt.

5 *Works*, 4:278. The ascription of these verses to Nero, derived from the ancient scholia and current in seventeenth-century editions (see *Works*, 4:665), has been doubted by some modern scholars, but is upheld by J. P. Sullivan, "Asses' Ears and *Attises:* Persius and Nero," *American Journal of Philology* 99 (1978): 159-70.

6 When the Romans talked about turning *pale*, they did not mean white but a yellowish-green hue. For some wonderfully literal-minded objections to "intus palleat" see *The Classical Papers of A. E. Housman*, ed. Diggle and Goodyear, 1:106-07, 110-11.)

7 William Empson, *Collected Poems* (New York: Harcourt, Brace and Co., 1949), p. 32.

8 So, I think, does Charles Tomlinson. See his *Poetry and Metamorphosis* (Cambridge: Cambridge Univ. Press, 1983), pp. 1-22.

9 Dryden noted: "The *Romans* were us'd to mark their Fortunate Days, or any thing that luckily befell 'em, with a White Stone which they had from the Island *Creta;* and their Unfortunate with a Coal." *Works*, 4:290. For example, in the beautiful and very moving sixty-eighth poem, Catullus says that he is not so foolish as to expect Lesbia to be faithful to him, "quare illud satis est, si nobis is datur unis / quem lapide illa diem candidiore notat," (therefore it is enough if she devotes solely to me the day which she marks with the whiter stone, 147-48).

10 *George Stepney's Translation of the Eighth Satire of Juvenal*, ed. Thomas Swendenberg and Elizabeth Swedenberg (Berkeley and Los Angeles: Univ. of California Press, 1948), p. 26.

11 I find it hard to understand how Reuben Brower, with the finest ear of any critic, could write: "A reader quite familiar with Dryden will find it impossible to distinguish Dryden's own translations of Juvenal from those of his helpers." "Seven Agamemnons," in *On Translation*, ed. Brower, p. 173.

12 "Quid enim tetrius quibusdam versibus Iuuenalis, propter quorum insolentiam vel iusserim vel optarim toto opere abstinere virum bonum?" (What indeed is more shameful than certain verses of Juvenal on account of which I would order or should hope that a good man would avoid his entire works?), Julius Caesar Scaliger, *Poetices libri septem* (Lyons, 1561), p. 378. This comment was often quoted in seventeenth-century editions.

13 "The peculiarity of Juvenal is a mixture of gaiety and stateliness, of pointed sentences, and declamatory grandeur. His points have not been neglected; but his grandeur none of the band seemed to consider as necessary to be imitated, except *Creech*, who undertook the thirteenth *satire*." Samuel Johnson, *Lives of the Poets*, 3 vols., ed G. Birkbeck Hill (Oxford: Clarendon Press, 1905), 1:447.

14 Gilbert Murray remarked: "Creech's versions of Horace and Theocritus may possess as little 'art of speech' as their famous critic implies—I speak without prejudice, never having seen them. They may be to us unreadable; bad verse in themselves, and full of Creech's tiresome personality, the Horace no Horace of ours, and the Theocritus utterly unlike Theocritus. But to Creech himself, how different it all was! He did not know how bad his lines were. He did not feel the veil of intervening Creech." *Euripides*, trans. Murray (London: George Allen & Unwin, 1902), pp. x-xi. Murray was misquoting Alexander Pope's *The Sixth Epistle of the First Book of Horace Imitated*, l. 2.

Ironically, Murray's translations of Euripides have probably sunk almost as low in critical esteem as Creech's Theocritus.

15 G. F. C. Plowden, in *Pope on Classic Ground* (Athens: Ohio Univ. Press, 1983), argues that Pope was heavily indebted to Creech's Manilius, but I am skeptical. See my review of Plowden's book in *Classical and Modern Literature* 4 (1984): 171-74.

Index